Figure 1. [Reconstruction drawing done by Michael Lewendon of his sighting of a massive vimana (UFO) over the AWE at Burghfield.]

MASSIVE VIMANA (UFO) OVER THE ATOMIC WEAPONS ESTABLISHMENT IN ENGLAND

A CHALLENGE FOR PARLIAMENT

Copyright © 2019 by Ananda L. Sirisena
The author's moral rights have been asserted.
All rights reserved. 3rd Edition 2019
ISBN 9781092328029

The Sanskrit word vi-māna (विमान) literally means "measuring out, traversing" or "having been measured out".

Vimana can be defined as "a car or a chariot of the gods, any self-moving aerial car sometimes serving as a seat or throne, sometimes self-moving and carrying its occupant through the air; other descriptions make the Vimana more like a house or palace or mansion, and one kind is said to be seven stories high", and quotes the Pushpaka Vimana of Ravana as an example.

It may denote any car or vehicle, especially a bier or a ship as well as a palace of an emperor, especially with seven stories.

In some Indian languages, vimana (or vimanam) means "aircraft", for example in the town name Vimanapura (a suburb of Bangalore) and Vimannagar, a town in Pune. In another context, Vimana is a feature in Hindu temple architecture.

Wikipedia

By the same author:

1) Co-author of "The Case For The Face - **Scientists Examine The Evidence For Alien Artifacts On Mars**"

2) Researcher for the book: **"UFOs - The Extraterrestrial Message"**

INTRODUCTION

Soon after my sighting of three 'flying discs' over south-west London on the 8th July 1964, I became very interested in the subject of "Unidentified Flying Objects" (UFOs). Little did I realise how life-enhancing that encounter with "flying saucers" would be. A detailed report of my sighting, which occurred in the presence of two school friends, appears in another chapter of this book. I started reading avidly around the subject and the whole debate about extraterrestrial life came into focus before my teenage eyes.

The realisation that these objects actually exist, burnt in my heart a deep yearning to understand their origins, their purpose and the motives of the greater intelligence behind the amazing power demonstrated to me on that sunny day. It made sense that if humans were to understand fully the phenomenon of Unidentified Flying Objects, then investigation of *claims of contact* was required.

And that investigation, apart from the physical study of these objects, had to be done in a scientific manner, with no assumptions or guessing about the motives of the claimants, or even the motives of the intelligences behind the 'saucers'. We need to understand any long term plan of advanced extraterrestrial beings who may be in control of spacecraft which have been observed in greater numbers since 1946. Each case of claimed contact had to be studied carefully and compared with other similar claims. Someone who claims contact with extraterrestrial intelligence is known as a "contactee".

This book covers primarily one 'contactee' although I do touch on several of the many other claims of contact. I have to use the words "claims of contact" because *proof* of any contact can be a personal one - personal to the investigator or investigators and not necessarily proof to the whole world. Indeed, the subject of universal proof and concepts behind such assertions are discussed at length in many academic studies - which is beyond the scope of this book.

If contact was made, then the 'claim or claims of contact' is true but then arises the question: "Did the claimant *later speak the truth about the contacts?"* Herein lies the thorny subject of truthful rendering of an experience. The reader is asked to decide on the results of my investigation of contactees and one British space contactee in particular –

Dr. George King, who founded the Aetherius Society in London, based on his attested claim of initial contact in 1954.

The first part of this book is about a spectacular sighting of a UFO over the Atomic Weapons Establishment (AWE) at Burghfield in the UK.

The second part covers the connection between the UFO phenomenon and nuclear sites, which has been documented by many researchers.

The third part considers the possibility that we might encounter many strange "artifacts" as we expand outwards into exploration of space towards the limits of our solar system. A couple of examples of such mysteries is detailed on the surface of Luna and Mars.

===

This author is currently President of the
Society For Planetary SETI Research (SPSR).

*[SETI = Search for Extraterrestrial Intelligence]

A web page for SPSR, at the University of Tennessee Space Institute (UTSI) can be found at the link below:

http://spsr.utsi.edu

Ananda L. Sirisena

Email: ANANDALS@AOL.COM

CONTENTS

PART 1 - The Report of an Unidentified Flying Object over the AWE

PART 2 - The Nuclear Connection

PART 3 - The Moon and Beyond......

PART 1

Chapter 1

The sighting on 11th September 2004

THE INITIAL REPORT

In 2010, a resident of Reading, in the county of Berkshire, contacted me with regard to a sighting that he had, together with his wife, six years earlier, in 2004. This sighting of a massive and rather unconventional looking object took place near the Atomic Weapons Establishment (AWE) at Burgfield. He is naturally concerned about the security aspects to our nation of this sighting. AWE used to be known as AWRE (Atomic Weapons Research Establishment) and is often referred to as Aldermaston. During the 1950's and 1960's world government programmes of atmospheric nuclear weapons testing, there were many peace marches, from and to Aldermaston, organised by the Campaign for Nuclear Disarmament (CND).

Both the witness and his wife clearly saw the very large, saucer-shaped object. The two of them observed this huge object *for well over 8 minutes* and saw it move towards the M4 motorway and in the direction of London. They are convinced that the object must have been captured on many cameras. The couple would like answers to the many questions raised by their astounding experience.

The primary witness is particularly worried about AWE security and strikes me as being a very patriotic person. There is nothing sinister in his wanting answers to so many questions that he has raised with myself and many others. Any reader who can offer the witness some solutions can offer positive suggestions by contacting the author. The witness has his own ideas about the origin of the UFO. Not one of us knows all the answers to the universal question of whether some UFOs represent visitation by a more advanced set of life forms from somewhere else in our solar system, or beyond, in our vast Galaxy - the Milky Way.

The Source of the Report

The source of this report, whom I shall refer to by his initials as ML, told me an extraordinary story about how one morning, around 6.30 - 7.00 am, he and his wife were returning home after babysitting at their daughter's house when they saw a huge object hovering over a field, to the right of the road that they were driving on. At the time of the sighting, it was a bright dawn with a clear, blue sky. ML had first spotted the object through the trees and whilst trying to keep it in sight, nearly drove into the ditch on the left-hand side of the road. His wife exclaimed to him to be careful, wondering why he was driving in such an erratic manner. He stopped the van and told his wife to look out through his window. He asked her, "What do you see?" She said, "What is it?!" He asked, "What does it look like?" **She said, "It looks like a spaceship!"**

Massive size of the 'saucer'

ML informed me that the object was, in his estimation, *many hundreds of feet in length*, with pastel coloured windows running through its centre, that appeared to pulsate on and off, due to the small clouds that were racing over them.. He found it difficult to explain that phenomenon and it is an astute observation, not just about the colour of its surface..

The couple observed the object for a short while, which ML estimated to be a few minutes, well over 5 minutes. He had alighted out of the van and climbed up on the bonnet (hood) to get a better look, as he could not see the bottom of the UFO. I asked ML to sketch the object. He was able to do this in a matter of a minute or so. I took him outside to look at the sky and asked him to give me an approximation of the *angle subtended* by the object. That is, it's length as it appeared to the naked eye, in the sky.

Many people may not be aware that it is difficult to assess the size of an object in the sky, unless one has a frame of reference, or a familiar object to compare it to nearby. One can compare the "apparent" size of an airborne object to the full moon and thus give some approximation to the angle subtended by the object. The full moon subtends half-a-degree. One could calculate the actual size of the object only if one knew the exact distance and altitude and the angle subtended to the eye. Two full moons, side by side, would subtend an angle of one degree.

First sketch

The figure below is the first sketch made by ML. It shows a classic "flying saucer" shape. The drawing was completed in a matter of a few seconds or so, without any hesitation, on the piece of paper I handed to him, together with a ballpoint pen.

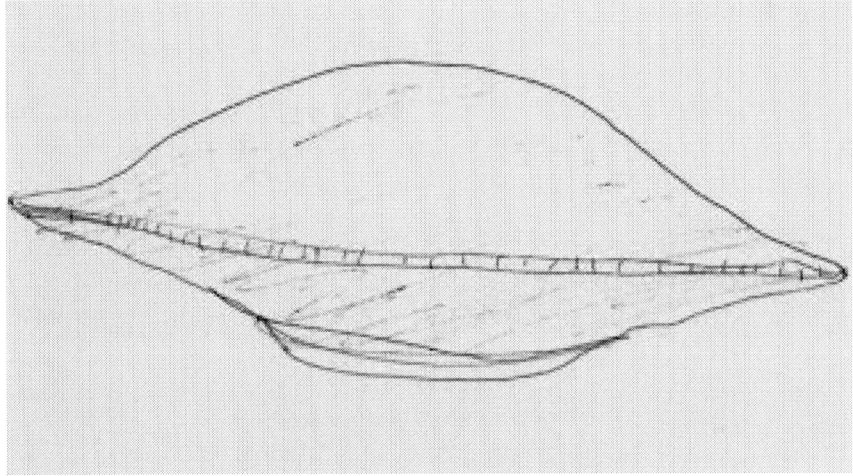

Figure 2 [Initial sketch made by ML the male witness]

When ML told me where he had stopped the van, I realised that they had been very close to a highly sensitive Ministry of Defence (MoD) property. The couple were just past Church Lane, (see the Figures 7 and 8) located on Burghfield Road, as it approached the M4 motorway, near the city of Reading. The massive object was hovering over a field adjacent to AWE—the Atomic Weapons Establishment at Burghfield. (The facility was previously known as AWRE, the Atomic Weapons Research Establishment.)

There are two sites there: AWE Aldermaston and AWE Burghfield
The UFO was very close to AWE Burghfield. Their website says:

"AWE Aldermaston covers a site of approximately 750 acres. Once a wartime airfield, today Aldermaston is a centre of excellence, housing advanced research, design and manufacturing facilities.

A former munitions factory, AWE Burghfield is a 225-acre site where warheads are assembled and maintained while in service, and decommissioned when out of service."

===
The website for AWE states:

"AWE plays a crucial role in the defence of the United Kingdom, by providing and maintaining the warheads for the country's nuclear deterrent. We are a centre of scientific and technological excellence, with some of the most advanced research, design and production facilities in the world."
===

The movement of the object

So ML and his wife had spotted what they called a "spaceship" next door to the Atomic Weapons Establishment. Suddenly, from a hovering position, the UFO started to move slowly around the MOD site, then towards the M4 motorway, heading easterly towards London. ML drove his van to the bridge that goes over the M4 motorway, stopped to observe the object and also noted many cars on the M4 driving in both directions, east towards London and west towards Bristol and Wales. [See Figures 7 and 8 on pages 25 & 26]

Lack of other witnesses

ML is convinced that there must have been many other witnesses because of the sheer size of the UFO and its proximity to AWE. He is certain that the object must have been captured on the innumerable **security cameras surrounding the site and wonders about the many other data recording instruments that would have archived the UFO visit.** He also wonders if the object was sighted by numerous drivers and their passengers on the M4 motorway as he recalls pointing at the UFO and noting many occupants of the vehicles looking towards it. It might even have possibly been picked up by the cameras that monitor traffic on that busy link between South Wales and London.

It was later established that the sighting had taken place on the 11th of September, 2004, England, postcode RG30 3TG at around 7.00am. It is odd, that when I first met them, the couple could not remember the exact date of their sighting. Nevertheless, I assured them that the first action we needed to do was to write down a brief report of their experience, regardless of not knowing the exact date.. What you have just read is the initial report, which was also published on the US-based website known as *"UFO Chronicles"* run by Frank Warren.

Identity revealed

As a 'UFO' investigator for many years, I usually do not reveal the names of witnesses in reports and use their initials for clarity, or give them a pseudonym. To my surprise. ML stated that he did not mind his name coming out into the public domain. Although he had not reported the sighting to any official body *at the time in 2004*, such as the police or the Ministry of Defence (MoD), he has been, in recent years, quite prolific in writing to many people in authority, trying to get answers to his many questions. So, ML is Michael Lewendon and his wife is Betty Lewendon. See Figure 5, page 14.

Radar and satellite tracking?

The couple had forgotten the *exact date* of the sighting but as a reference, mentioned that there had been a report in a newspaper, a few days after their sighting, of another UFO sighting. Whilst ML appreciates that this case is not "news" after so many years, he would like some kind of official confirmation of his sighting. He feels that the UFO must have been tracked on radar, been seen by satellite, and visually observed by many other people.

In a serendipitous happening, the couple needed to renew a passport for some holiday travel and by chance, found the original scrap of paper on which Betty, had written a note on a magazine cover *the day after the sighting*. The colour magazine cover is shown below, after its discovery with an old passport that needed renewal. This pinpointed not only the exact date but also the approximate time of the majestic sighting, noted contemporaneously.

MASSIVE VIMANA OVER THE AWE

Figure 3

[Cover page of a magazine dated 12 September 2004, on which Betty Lewendon had scrawled the words "Space Ship" and the date and time of the sighting of the massive UFO over the AWE, Burghfield. This piece of paper was initially misplaced and found later.]

It's a spaceship

His wife Betty, is equally mystified by the appearance of this object. Her first reaction was that it was a 'spaceship' and she has not changed her opinion since that day. What was it doing hovering over a highly sensitive MOD site? Did the armed guards at AWE spot it? Where did it come from? Where did it go? There are many intriguing questions which do need answers.

US military revelations

It is a fact that the Pentagon, US military headquarters, in December 2017, released information about several sightings made by military pilots from the USS Nimitz in 2004, during exercises off the California coast. These reports and corresponding interviews with the pilots have been documented on TV and radio, many times since. Any reader can look up AATIP on the internet and find several interviews with the pilots and see the films.

That was the first time that the US military acknowledged the existence of unidentified flying objects - in December, 2017, despite controversy about the subject being in place since June 1947, when the expression "Flying Saucer" was coined and since the early days of US military investigation. It has been stated by several investigators that Brazil and France were the first nations to officially admit to the presence of unconventional aerial vehicles in their skies.

The US Air Force projects Sign, Grudge and Blue Book were part of the US military engagement with the public of the USA and the whole world. Project Blue Book was closed down in early 1969, upon the recommendation of the University of Colorado which conducted a study into UFOs, known as the "Condon Report" and made its summary available in the latter part of 1968. It should be noted here, that the Condon Report could not provide answers for over a third of the reports it studied. Its summary was at variance with this genuine failure to account for such a large proportion of the cases investigated.

Many ufo researchers have carefully scrutinised the way the Condon Report was produced. Such studies are available freely so will not be considered here.

ADDENDUM TO THE REPORT - UFO SIGHTED NEAR BRITISH NUCLEAR WEAPONS FACILITY - An extraordinary account

Rushing clouds inside the object

I met the witness again in December 2016 and we revisited the site of the observation of the massive object near and above the AWE (Atomic Weapons Establishment), which took place on 11th. September 2004.

The witness ML – Michael Lewendon, stated that, **"The thunderous-looking clouds were rushing through the object, as if it was a form of camouflage. But the sky was blue - not a cloud in the sky anywhere. The rushing clouds gave the impression, together with the pastel coloured lights, that the object was spinning. There must have been** over 40 or more pastel coloured lights forming a band in the middle of the object, so huge was the UFO. (See front cover)

"I felt privileged, felt as if I was gifted to see such an event. Phew, from being scared one minute to amazement in my heart! The craft was hovering 50 yards away, about 200 feet in the air."

The sheer size of the object!

Michael estimates the craft to have been 100 - 200 metres (328 feet - 656 feet) across and 30 metres (98 feet) deep, with a hint of a dome on top. It could have been larger he estimates, always being conservative. He is used to estimating distances, based on his previous job. When I tested his powers of size estimation, he got the length of a nearby wall guessed to within a few inches - high accuracy, without a doubt!
[See Michael's drawing on the cover of the book for sheer perspective]

After getting out of his van, observing the saucer-shaped object for a full five to seven minutes, during which time he tooted the horn several times to try and awaken nearby residents, the object started to move. No one else came to view it and strangely, no other cars passed by during those few minutes. Apart from the car horn noise, there was total silence. Michael has wondered whether the sound of the horn was recorded somewhere?

As far as he knows, he and his wife were the only witnesses to this grand object in the sky at the time, who have come forward. Michael says it is quite a busy road and there is constant traffic on it, so he is perplexed as to why no other cars passed by during their eight-minute observation. He asked me if they might have been in some kind of time-tunnel? I do not know the answer to that reasonable question. Researchers have concluded that within proximity of the "force screens" surrounding UFOs, there might be distortions of time and space. Such a probability cannot be discounted, even if we do not fully understand the physics behind the propulsion systems of such craft. He said:

Observe and memorise

"I decided to tell myself to remember every detail, as I was seeing something that was going to be investigated and my information could be of great significance"

"I had time to place an article by a road sign, which I recovered a few days later, just in case we were somewhere else - the article was still there!

"The ship moved off, in an arc shape to our left, going up as it moved. Its path took it straight over the atomic research base, 500 yards away and then it went parallel to the M4 motorway, towards London. That is where we lost sight of the ship. I drove up the road to the bridge which goes over the M4 and parked the van again to see if there was anything I could add to this ufo sighting."

Lost opportunity by our government

Michael is perplexed at the lack of investigation by the authorities. He wrote, some years after the event, to the then British Prime Minister, David Cameron, hoping to receive some acknowledgement of his report. He received no reply. He even wrote to the Gracious Queen of England, hoping to hear about some sort of investigation by some official body. He is convinced that the traffic cameras covering the motorway would have picked up the object, as well as the myriad of security cameras around the AWE. He asks, **"What about weather stations, the BBC, satellite imagery and Google Earth?"**

He tells me, **"I do really want any report to concentrate on the reluctance of the government to investigate. This was no little light in the sky at night. It was not for a few seconds, this "thing" was huge and massive, larger than Wembley stadium.** *It could have been occupied by hundreds of thousands of people.* **In total my wife and I observed this "spaceship" for over 8 minutes. I need your write-up of our sighting to confront the powers that have the ability to investigate, to go through official archives and come up with an answer. It will be the same results, as if we saw this yesterday. We need to tell the people that I have tried to get an investigation - but who has the power to initiate this?"**

They never harmed us

"This goes down in history as the biggest missed chance to reproduce that day's events. *They came here to do something, change something, leave something. They never bothered about me and Betty, they never harmed us.* The whole point about this is that it never got investigated. There must be evidence in official archives that indicate we might have been in some sort of "time warp". Instruments in and around this area will show distortions of time and space, some kind of a tunnel. If they look, they will find all we saw. There's a national security risk for one thing because this "UFO" was hovering over the Atomic Weapons facility. This has implications for space travel, this knowledge belongs to mankind and our children's children; these archives will show that space travel exists."

Michael's frustration about the lack of an official response led him to write a children's story about their encounter, which he sent to Prince Charles at Buckingham Palace. He hopes the Prince of Wales will read the story to his grandchildren.

The Crescent Moon

Michael remembers that on this bright morning, before sunrise, he saw the crescent of the moon, with a "very bright" light, like a bright star, close to it. Initially he thought that bright light was the International Space Station (ISS) but now he is sure it was the planet Venus. The ISS would have been moving. The 'bright star' was not moving at the time but maintained an apparently constant relationship with the moon, during the duration of the event.

I used an astronomical computer programme to check the sky between 6 - 6.30 am on the 11th September 2004. It clearly shows that there was a crescent moon in the sky, with the planet Venus, shining below the tip of the moon. Michael Lewendon is indeed a very observant witness.

Figure 4. [In the stellarium view shown above, the Moon is close to Venus in the sky. Also visible are the planets Mercury and Saturn just before sunrise, after 6.00 am, although these planets would not have been as bright or clear as the Moon and Venus.]

Figure 5 [The witnesses : Betty and Mick Lewendon]

CHAPTER 2

INTERVIEW WITH BETTY LEWENDON

Q. Please go back to that date and tell me the story in your own words, what happened....why were you on the road at 6.00 am?

A. We had stayed over at our daughter's house in Burghfield for the night. We were coming back home. That is when we see this object.

Q. Did you spot it first?

A. Not really. I asked Mick why was he driving so erratically and he pulled over the van at the time. And he looked and he said, "What's that?" And I said, "It looks like a spaceship!" And then after a while it went.......

Q. Was it stationary to begin with? How long for?

A. Yes, it was stationary. Hard to tell really, observed it for some minutes. Then it went over towards Whitley, I would say...

Q. Did you hear any sound?

A. No. Nothing at all.

Q. What was your impression of the size of the object?

A. It was BIG! Mick couldn't believe it. He said, "What is that?" I said again: "It's a spaceship".

Q. Did Mick get out of the van?

A. Yes he did. By that time the object had started moving. It was hovering over the field to begin with. Mick got out and stood on the van trying to get a better look.

Q. You saw him doing that? At anytime did you feel like getting out of the van yourself?

A. Yes I saw all that. I did not want to get out of the van. I just wanted Mick to go - just go, get home.

Q. Were you frightened?

A. Not really. It's just that it was something you haven't seen before and you don't really understand it, do you?

Q. How would you describe it to me?

A. Round shape. Lights going around it as well.

Q. Would you be able to sketch it for me?

A. Yes. And it seemed to be spinning.

[See sketch made by Betty Lewendon, independently of Michael]

SKETCH MADE BY BETTY LEWENDON OF OBJECT SEEN ON 11 SEPT. 2004

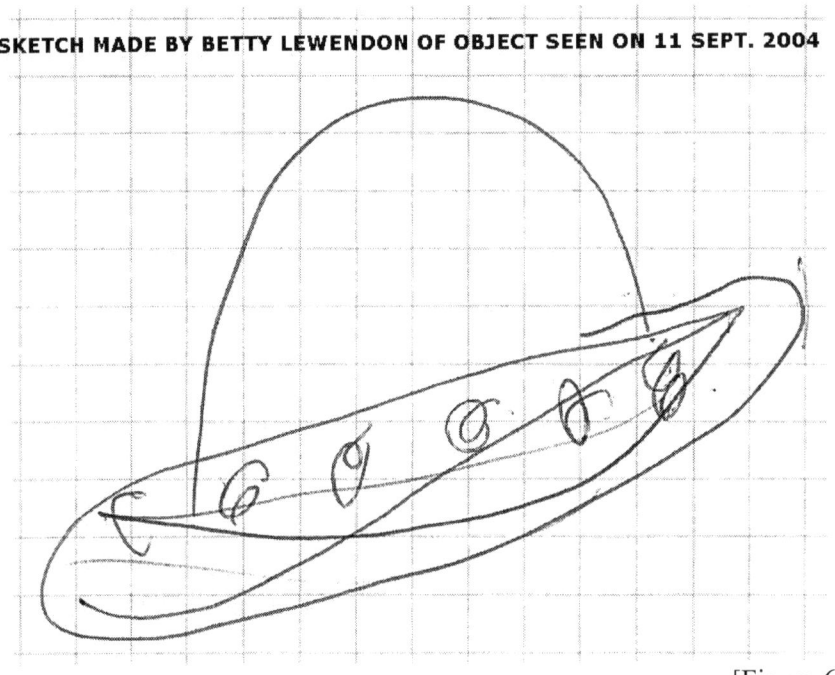

[Figure 6]

Q. What colour was it - the object?

A. A grey colour.

Q. Was there anything on the top of the object?

A. I couldn't see nothing.

Q. Were there many lights on the body of the object?

A. Quite a few. Because I was so shocked I didn't really notice details like that. But the lights were going round it, spinning.

Q. Were the lights of different colours?

A. The lights were not all one colour - the object a greyish, cloudy colour.

Q. The object you said was a grey colour - but were the lights a different colour?

A. They were just shining!

Q. Mick said the object was stationary over the field, then went up in the air slowly, moving at first towards the AWE, then towards the M4 motorway.

A. Yes. Then he got back in the van, after having tooted the horn and drove towards the bridge that goes over the M4.

Q. When he stopped on the bridge that goes over the M4, did you remain in the van?

A. I stayed in the van. He got out again.

Q. At that stage did you see it?

A. Yes. But there was no sound at all, from it.

Q. Were you amazed, that such a huge object, whilst moving, did not make any sound? Any whirring, any humming sound?

A. Yes I was amazed. No sound at all. Hmmm....and it was my mum's birthday the next day and I said to her about it and she was so amazed! I told her what I had seen.

Q. So she was interested in what you had seen and reported to her?

A. Yeah, she was so amazed.

Q. What did she say?

A. Well, she was amazed. When you speak to people now they don't believe you, do they?

Q. Many people do believe reports of sightings. I am interested to know what you felt? Did you feel any fear? Any awe?

A. I don't know. Mixed feelings really. I didn't feel any fear. I was just amazed as to what it could be. Was there anyone in it? How did it get there? How did it take off? How is it up there? These were the sort of questions going through my mind.

Q. Could there have been many "people" in there - in the object?

A. I don't know. We didn't even know what it is, did we?

Q. Are you any good at estimating distance or size of objects?

A. No, not at all.

Q. You said it was huge. Do you think it was large enough, if it was a spaceship, to hold many "space people"?

A. Yeah. I didn't know how big it was - just that it was big enough for us to see clearly. I was amazed really at what it could be.

Q. So you were looking out through the right hand side window of the van?

A. Yes, I'm sat there in the passenger seat. Mick is now outside. Looking out that way. We are parked on the left side of the road.

Q. When you first saw it, how high did it appear to be, off the ground?

A. At first, it wasn't very high. Until it started drifting. No sound, just amazed. I said: "What is that?" That is when Mick stopped the van. He stopped and said, "Don't know".

Q. Did it appear as large as the full moon?

A. I don't really know. You don't expect to see something like that in the sky at six in the morning. It may have been as large as three full moons together.

Q. Was it a bright clear morning. Did you spot the moon?

A. Yes, it was bright. No I did not see the moon. I didn't get out. All I said after that, was, when we get home, let's phone the *Evening Post* and tell them. "No, no." said Mick, "No, no. They'll think we are crazy."

Q. Is that what Mick said at the time?

A. (Laughing....) We don't drink.....so it wasn't cause of that, as if anyone could have accused us of that.

Q. So you would have happily spoken to a reporter that day?

A. There was a report earlier, can't remember whether it was the *Evening Post* or not.....

Q. And then you forgot about it?

A. Yeah. We just forgot about it. Well, you know it wouldn't have mattered if we went to the AWRE. The AWE are not going to say anything to you - because it's all private there.

Q. Well, it is a Ministry of Defence site, regulated by the Official Secrets Act. After all, the AWE is the Atomic Weapons Establishment! That is where they do research on atomic weapons.

A. Obviously, on their radar they would have picked up the object. Because they have planes, don't they? In case anything does happen. I know there was no sound from it but they must have been able to see it on the cameras. They must have some record, they must have seen it on the cameras. But Mick wasn't interested in reporting it at the time. Which I can understand, because it's private and all that.

Q. Who else did you tell?

A. Just my mum - the next day. When you do tell people, gee -- they look at you! People weren't really interested. It was the day before my mum's birthday, because I went to see her next day, the 12th. That piece of paper, the magazine cover scrap we gave you, was proof that we did see it and that I documented it at the time.

Q. Since that sighting, have you thought about it a lot?

A. No, not a lot. It was one of those things for me. But not for Mick really, but for me it was one of those things.

Q. You said it's a "spaceship". That implies it came through space from somewhere else, maybe another planet?

A. We don't really know. I've seen on TV a lot of these programmes about spaceships...

Q. On any of those TV programmes, have you seen something similar?

A. Yeah. About the same or similar. It was spinning when it was going away but very quiet - it made no noise! We can't really say how big it was.

Q. Can you compare its size to several full moons?

A. I don't really know. At least three or four....It was BIG. Drifted then disappeared off towards the Whitley area..

Q. I did write to the local MP, who received a reply from the AWE. Since that time in 2004 have you felt anything else resulting from your experience?

A. No.

Q. And you state that it did not harm you in any way?

A. No it did not harm us.

Q. You happened to be on that road at that time....

A. Luckily enough! I did wonder why it was there - over the AWE.

Q. In using the word 'spaceship' presumably you thought it was a craft that was not from Earth - am I correct?

A. Yes that is right.

Q. Did you wonder about the sheer size of the object?

A. I wondered - "Is there anyone in there?" How does that thing stay aloft? A lot of people are not interested.

==
==

In case readers are wondering why the sketch made by Betty Lewendon appears to be different from that made by her husband Michael Lewendon it is worth noting that we all perceive things somewhat differently. Betty Lewendon did not get out of the van at the time. From two different perspectives and viewing points the same object may have appeared slightly different. Also, if witnesses are not artistically trained then their drawings will be somewhat basic and not detailed. Both sketches were rendered very quickly. They were not given time to think about their drawings.

CHAPTER 3

As the witness, Michael Lewendon feels a great deal of frustration about not receiving replies from any official body, I wrote to the local MP (Member of Parliament). My attempts to contact AWE directly, even the security department there met with no success. It is as if nobody wanted to talk to a "ufo researcher" about somebody else's sighting. This was not about my sighting but about the Lewendon's report. I realised the importance of this one sighting because of its proximity to the AWE and possible security implications.

Letter to MP from the AWE

Eventually, the local MP received a letter from the Chief Executive at AWE. The letter, marked "Official", is reproduced below. Several interesting talking points arise from this official letter. If I had not written to the local MP, then we would have had no reply from any official body. The fact that the letter does not acknowledge a ufo presence on the date of 11th September, 2004, above AWE at Burghfield, is to be expected. It is not really surprising, considering the sceptical attitude towards the subject by many in the scientific community. Perhaps, now that the US military is more open about sightings, such as from the USS Nimitz in 2004, we might eventually be more open in the UK, regardless of the fact that the MoD has released entire directories of sighting reports going back many decades.

I have redacted the letter only to remove the names of the Member of Parliament and the Chief Executive at AWE. Some of the paragraphs from the letter are worth discussing in detail later.

Letter received by the Member of Parliament from AWE

22 May 2017

Aldermaston • Reading
Berkshire • RG7 4PR
Tel: 0118 981 4111

House of Commons
London
SW1A 0AA

RECEIVED 3 0 MAY 2017

Thank you for your letter of 24 January regarding a query from one of your constituents describing a possible UFO sighting near AWE Aldermaston.
As you can imagine, AWE has long been the subject of various examples of lurid speculation and rumour. I believe that we are regarded by some as a likely point of interest and interaction for extra-terrestrial activity, due to the nature of our work, but there is no credible evidence to support this view.
Investigating the source of the incident reported by your constituent, we discovered that the text of the letter had appeared previously on a website called the UFO Chronicles. This site features reports of UFO sightings and information on CIA conspiracies, alien abductions and alien activity. The report was written by Ananda Sirisena in 2010 and appeared on the UFO Chronicles website in December 2016.

I can confirm that we are not aware of any UFO sightings or activity at AWE Aldermaston. As you may know, the Ministry of Defence formerly recorded all reports of UFO sightings from across the UK but this function (the so-called 'UFO Desk') was discontinued in 2009.

As AWE is run on behalf of the UK Government and MOD owns our sites, I am confident that we would have been made aware of any UFO-related information relevant to our operations or premises.

There is a surprising amount of official material relating to claims about UFOs which your constituent may enjoy researching. They will be able to find information on all sightings reported to the MOD between 1997 and 2009 at https://www.gov.uk/government/publications/ufo-reports-in-the-uk. These reports include dates and times, location and a brief description of the sighting.

The second page of the letter from the Chief Executive is reproduced here also. The MP had written to AWE in January 2017 and the reply to him, as can be seen, is dated 22nd May, 2017 - a 4-month delay in replying.

The National Archives also contains a wide range of UFO-related documents, drawings, letters, photos and parliamentary questions, covering the final two years of the Ministry of Defence's UFO Desk (from late 2007 until November 2009).

These can be found at http://www.nationalarchives.gov.uk/ufos/

I hope this is of assistance to your constituent,

Yours sincerely

Chief Executive

The AWE letter states: *"AWE has long been the subject of lurid speculation and rumour"*. This is an unnerving claim. I have never seen "lurid" claims about the AWE anywhere. I have read newspaper reports about the AWE which have been detailed. Most of the news reports deal with day to day activities of the establishment.

The Chief Executive of the AWE states, *"I believe that we are regarded by some as a likely point of interest and interaction for extraterrestrial activity....."*.

This author wonders why the Chief Executive would say something like that? We were just trying to report a sighting of a very large object hovering, then moving over the AWE. Neither Michel Lewendon or his wife Betty made any speculations as such. Both of them feel very patriotic towards our country and wish to have some explanations about their sightings. They are rightly worried about possible threats to a military establishment, not very far from where they reside. They are law-abiding citizens of the UK and have valid concerns about safety and security. They feel that our military, the Royal Air Force and radar detection sites are a valuable part of the nation's defences and hold the military in high esteem. Both of them are shocked that their report has simply been brushed under a carpet of disinterest and scepticism.

The Chief Executive also says: *"As AWE is run on behalf of the UK Government and MOD owns our sites, I am confident that we would have been made aware of any UFO-related information relevant to our operations or premises"*

Is it possible that this very large 'vimana' had been totally undetected - by radar, satellite imagery or photographic surveillance?

If that is the case, then the UFO had remarkable ability to evade detection. It must have slipped under our umbrella of detection and protection. That fact alone should be of great concern to all authorities, including Members of Parliament. Or someone has not informed the Chief Executive of what may have been tracked officially. That is also concerning.

Haunted skies

Sightings of unidentified flying objects over the AWE have been occurring over many decades. Several reports from and around Reading, in the county of Berkshire, are published in a series of books, entitled "Haunted Skies".

I have received several reports from residents in and around Reading over the years. Since the elusive UFOs do not hover around for too long, it is difficult to state definitively, from a scientific perspective, as to their nature and origin. Many a researcher around the world has found traces where objects have *landed on the ground* but in this particular instance the behemoth object was hovering over a field before moving towards the buildings of the AWE and then towards London, on a path parallel to the M4 motorway.

There are many radar-visual reports from around the world; i.e. reports of sightings seen visually by one or more witnesses whilst being tracked simultaneously on radar. There are also visual sightings that were not tracked on radar - almost as though these objects have a switch in them that can be turned on or off for radar evasion. We have developed technology to evade radar, so it should not surprise us to see it in a potentially more advanced spacecraft from elsewhere.

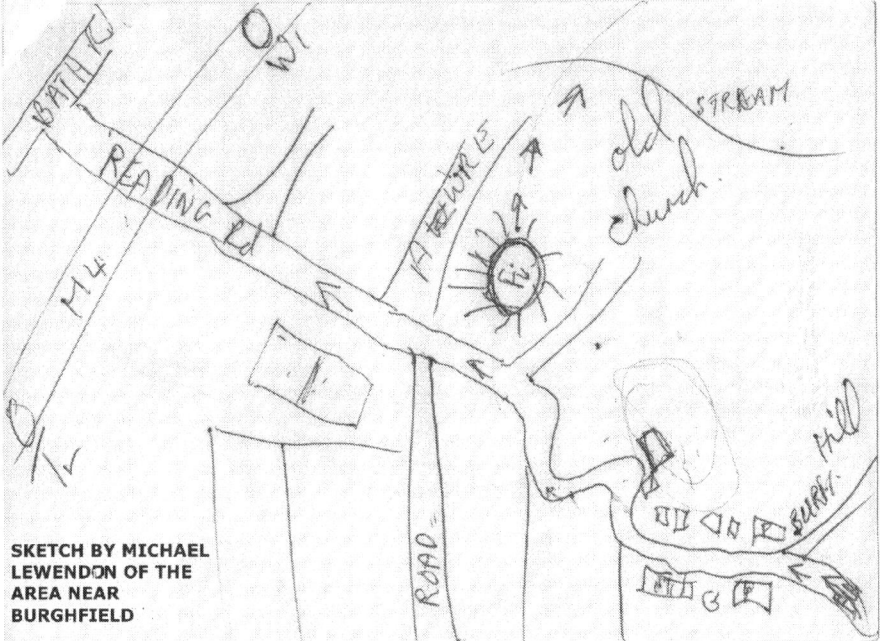

Figure 7

Michael Lewendon provided me with several more maps of the area, on which he highlighted the direction that the object had taken, towards Shire Hall. The fact that it was so close to the AWE is concerning, as the object was not a conventional terrestrial craft. If it was an enemy observational craft one would expect that it had been detected by military radar but it seems that this particular 'flying saucer' had entered our airspace by evading radar detection and was openly moving, in a casual-flowing and carefree manner.

The church indicated on the map is still there as I write this in 2019. Michael Lewendon had first stopped his van just near a triangular patch of grass which was in the centre of two roads diverting. He was so astonished at what he was seeing that he got out of the van and eventually stood on top of the bonnet of the van, to get a closer look. Throughout the sighting, neither he nor his wife heard any sound from the object. He felt that the surroundings were quiet but when he pressed the horn on the van he definitely heard the very loud toot.

Later, he wondered why no other cars passed in either direction on what is usually a busy road, even at that time in the early hours of the morning.

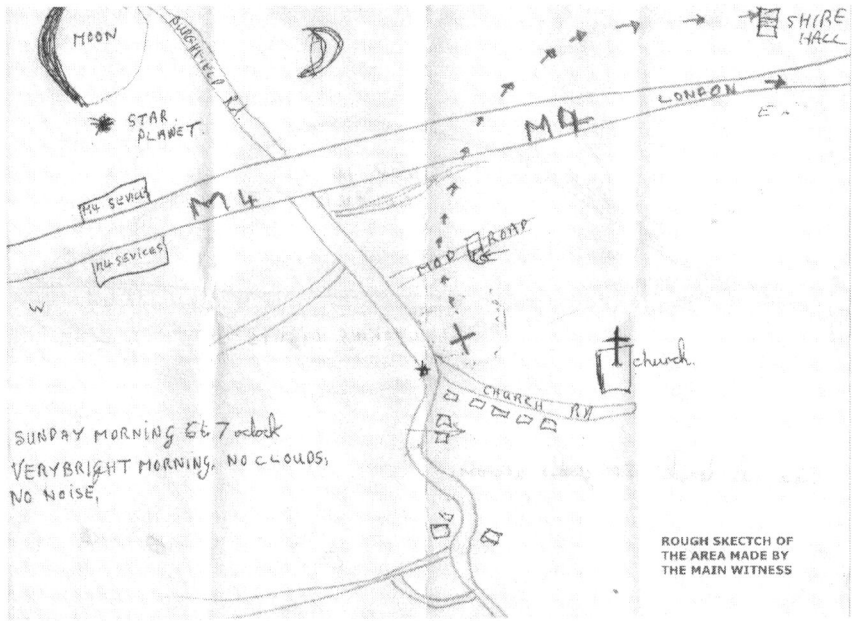

Figure 8

[Two sketches made by ML of the area near the AWE sighting]

The object went from a hovering position over a field near Church Road and ultimately towards the M4 motorway. Michael felt it was moving in the direction of Shire Hall but cannot be certain exactly where it went out of sight although it flew parallel to the M4 motorway for some distance. When he stopped on the bridge at the M4 he saw cars travelling on the motorway and started pointing at the object. He is convinced that the occupants of several cars looked at what he was pointing at and also saw the object.

So it is possible that there were other witnesses to the circular craft who have not come forward and probably never thought of reporting their sightings to any official body - just like Mick and Betty had not reported it to anyone on the day of their sighting. Effectively, they 'sat on' their sighting report until they even forgot exactly what day it had happened.

[The series of books called "HAUNTED SKIES" reports several sightings near, or over Aldermaston and the AW(R)E, going back many decades].

Local news papers in Reading have published UFO reports from time to time. Although we did not find the report dating back to the week of September 2004, here are some other Berkshire articles.

From the Reading Weekend Post, Friday 25 August 2006

UFO SIGHTINGS?: unexplained lights have been seen all over Reading. Is it a bird, is it a plane? Who knows but it's there.
More sightings of UFOs over the skies of Reading have flooded into the *Evening Post.*
The reports follow an article on Monday describing how Avarind Donohoe saw strange lights above his house in Newtown on Saturday night.
Maxine Webb, of Walton Close, Woodley, called in to tell us she managed to catch the action on her camcorder on Saturdy night.
She said, "It was really strange, there were about six lights that were mushroom-shaped that travelled through the sky, then came together before they went out.
"We watched them for a while as they were travelling really slowly. It was unexplainable."
Jordan Atkinson,12, of Coventry road, Newtown, was out playing with friends when he also saw the lights on Saturday.
He said, "They were an orangey colour and we saw one, then we saw another three that formed a triangle and later some more. We were watching them for about 15 minutes before they disappeared. My friend looked at them through binoculars and said they looked like balls of fire."
But it seems the strange action was not just on Saturday night.
Jean Hodgson, 81, of Wyndham Crescent, Woodley, was sitting in bed in the early hours of Wednesday August 1, at about 2am, when she saw some unusual activity. She said: "It literally looked like a cluster of stars but it was pulsating.
"There were two lights outside a circle of lights and it came towards me really slowly before going over the house. I had a good look and I hadn't even been drinking anything."
One suggestion for the strange sights was meteor activity that astronomers have said is likely to be visible this month from the Perseids Shower.
But amateur astronomer Steve Harris, from Newbury Astronomical Society, said the descriptions did not match what he would have expected people to see. He said, "Meteors only last for a couple of seconds and although they do sometimes travel in groups, it is not very common.
"The more likely explanation is that it is space debris that has entered the atmosphere but it is strange that it was sighted on more than one occasion. I would think it was probably an aeroplane flying through low cloud."
Ananda Sirisena, one of Britain's leading ufologists, believes that it is highly likely that another 'life form' exists, said: "It is hard to judge these

things without seeing it directly but it does suggest intellectual control as the formations described seem very structured."

Actually, what I said to newspaper reporter was: "It does suggest "intelligent" control, not "intellectual" control." And I said that some ufos do show a definite structure. I was referring to actual objects, as opposed to any formation that they make. In the first couple of these reports, a strong possibility is that the witnesses saw Chinese lanterns; they did not report a definite structure. The triangular *formation* could have resulted from three lighted lanterns being released one after the other in quick succession. They were said to move very slowly, just as Chinese lanterns would - with the wind and they tend to move upwards until their flame dies and seem to vanish suddenly. But we cannot know for sure what they saw. The 'orangey' colour and 'balls of fire' seen through binoculars do strongly suggest Chinese lanterns.

However, witness Jean Hodgson, wrote me several letters. What she described to me did not look like a Chinese lantern. She said,
"I have found it terribly difficult to draw what I saw and I think I may have put in too many lights even now! As our house is cock-eyed to the compass, you will see my first sighting was from the south. The lights were equidistant and of unusual colour. When I first saw them they were a small cluster but bigger than the moon when they were close.
"One of my family looked you up one her computer; so I went to the library to see if I could get a book you had written but had no luck. If you have written one I would love to read it, so would you be kind enough to let me know it's name so that I can order it? It is all very weird and exciting!"

A second letter stated:

"Dear Mr. Sirisena,
  Surprise, surprise. I didn't think I would see my cluster of lights again but I did again at 2.20am, the night we changed our clocks. This time they weren't coming towards me but moved very rapidly and flashing very rapidly from right to left and then left to right and disappeared behind large trees at each end of the run - MADDENING!. I really am amazed but know that I am not seeing things.
    Yours sincerely, Jean Hodgson."

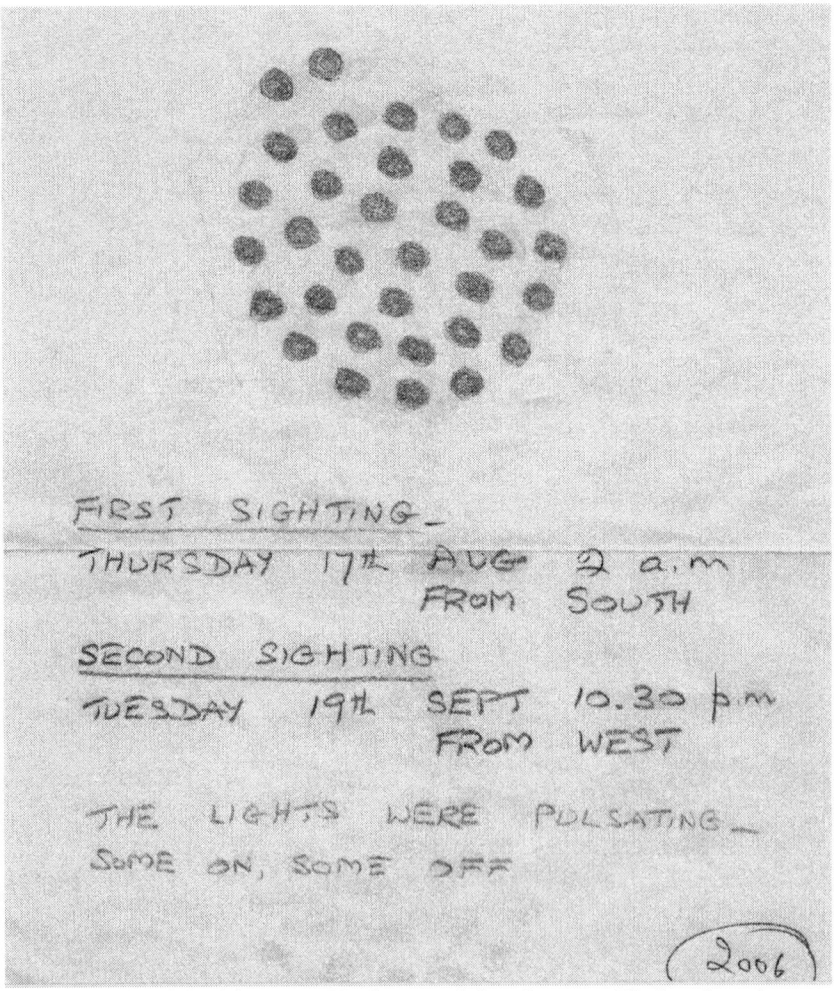

[Drawing furnished by Jean Hodgson of the cluster of lights that she saw on more than one occasion]

From the Reading Evening Post - Friday 16 May 2008

"Hot spot for UFOs - it's official "

Flying saucers, bright white lights and other strange objects have been seen flying above Reading, according to new files released by the Ministry of Defence (MoD).
The previously secret files were opened this week and detail people's reports of spotting unidentified flying objects (UFOs) in the sky.
The 'X-files' includes information dating back to the 1970s and the MoD's evaluations of the information it received.

And Reading seems to be a hot spot for these peculiar sightings, with the town having several mentions in the files.
In June 1997, one Woodley householder reported "numerous, ball-shaped, white lights".
The spotter added: "They were high in the sky, rapid, moving horizontal and round and round and up and down".
Two months later, a "hovering red light, with a strong white light coming from it" was spotted in Arborfield.
Meanwhile, a year later, a 28ft circular object, with a dome on top which sported a "bright yellowish/whitish light" was seen over the skies of Finchhampstead.
And the eerie sightings do not stop there, with one person claiming he saw an object with approximately 300 tentacles somewhere in Reading.
Leading British UFO investigator Ananda Sirisena, from Caversham, said the number of sightings in the town have remained steady and he has received around half a dozen reports in the area in the past year.
He said: "There have been several reports from different areas of Reading.
"People are quite sincere when they report what they have seen. I have noticed that they do not exaggerate, they are mystified and would like to know what it is they have seen."
Mr. Sirisena, who became interested in extra-terrestrial investigation after he saw a UFO himself in the summer of 1964 on his way to school, is a leading authority on the subject and will be giving a talk on the MoD's file release at the Inner Potential Centre in London on Wednesday.
He told the *Evening Post* that while the MoD's move is a step in the right direction, more needs to be done to raise the profile of UFO sightings in the country.
Mr. Sirisena said: "It's about time the files were released. But they should release all the classified military reports as well. It's a gradual breakthrough which should have been taking place for a long time."
He added: "This is an indication that people do see unusual things and do report them. Hopefully scientists will now start to appreciate the subject with a more open mind."
The MoD said its files had more to do with monitoring UK security and releasing files in a structured way, given the large number of requests it gets each year for information on UFOs, than playing Mulder and Scully.
A spokesman for the MoD said: "To date, independent experts have concluded that there are realistic explanations behind alleged UFO reports, such as aircraft lights or natural phenomena.
"Reports are examined by the Ministry of Defence solely to establish whether UK airspace may have been compromised by hostile or unauthorised military activity.

"If required, sighting reports are examined with the assistance of the department's air defence experts.

"Unless there is evidence of a potential threat, no further works are undertaken to identify the nature of each sighting reported.

The Ministry of Defence has no other interest or role regarding UFO matters and does not consider questions regarding the existence or otherwise of extra-terrestrial life."

The released files can be seen on The National Archives website at: http://ufos.nationalarchives.gov.uk

The files will be available to download free for the first month, after which the National Archives will charge for them.

The rest of the files are currently under review and will be added to the National Archives over the next three years.

*   *

AWE Aldermaston: Nuclear weapons factory fined £1m
The UK's nuclear weapons factory has been fined £1m for failing to ensure the safety of its staff.

An electrician suffered burns to his arm in June 2017, while carrying out routine testing at the Atomic Weapons Establishment (AWE) in Berkshire.

The prosecution was brought by the UK's independent nuclear safety watchdog, the Office of the Nuclear Regulator.

AWE said it "deeply regrets" the injury to the member of staff and it did not meet its "usually high standards".

An investigation into the injury in 2017 by the Office for Nuclear Regulation (ONR) deemed it to be a health and safety matter and there was no radiological risk to workers or the public.

Pleaded guilty
Nuclear inspectors had raised concern about the safety of staff involved in this test work two years earlier.

Donald Urquhart, of the ONR, said: "We welcome today's outcome which recognises that AWE fell short in its duty to protect a worker."

In a statement, AWE said a full review of electrical safety processes and systems across the AWE sites had since been carried out, with "actions being taken to minimise the risk of recurrence".

The Aldermaston site is responsible for making Britain's Trident nuclear warheads and stores nuclear waste from Royal Navy submarines.

AWE had previously pleaded guilty to the offences under the Health and Safety at Work Act at Reading Magistrates' Court.

It was also ordered to pay costs of £26,096.

The above report was published by the BBC on 9th November 2018. The AWE is often in the local news. Publicity about the site is factually reported and there is no 'lurid' speculation.

===

MY FORAY INTO UFOLOGY

How and why did I become a UFO investigator? This question has been asked of me several times, by many people who know me well and wonder what is my fascination with a subject regarded as weird and their impression is that it is quite often the playing fields of cranks, eccentrics and charlatans..

In order to answer their question sincerely, I placed a 14-minute narration on a YouTube channel called **"The Day Three Flying Saucers Came To Wimbledon"**, the text of some of which is reproduced below. It is a truthful account of a personal sighting that triggered my interest in the subject of unidentified flying objects or "flying saucers".

Were it not for my sighting I might probably not have taken such an interest in the subject. However, I would say honestly that I do not think I would have heaped ridicule on witnesses who have come forward. **I do not think that it is scientific to laugh at, or deride witnesses who are simply reporting what they have seen. Ridicule, laughter and derision are not signs of a mature mind and no scientist should ever disregard witness observations. After all, much of scientific progress has been based on "observation". Modern astronomy would not exist were it not for observation. I urge all "sceptical" scientists to retain an open mind. There is a difference between "healthy scepticism" and an unhealthy, cavalier dismissal of witness statements simply as "just anecdotes". Remember, "stones cannot fall from the sky" said some years ago by prominent scientists.**

THREE DISCS ON 8th JULY 1964

Something very strange and unexpected happened to me on the 8th July 1964. I was on my way to school in south-west London, England, with two of my friends, when we saw three 'flying discs' in the sky. It was a bright, sunny morning with white fluffy clouds being driven by a slow and steady breeze. The three of us were walking along the road at about 08.50 am, engaged in a scholarly discussion about the merits of the song-writing of the Beatles versus the raucous singing of the Rolling Stones. Or we might have been extolling the pugilistic skills of one Muhammad Ali who had recently changed his name from Cassius Clay and was creating a sensation in the world of heavyweight boxing.

Suddenly, a "mental hook" pulled my eyes upwards. I stopped walking and talking - in utter amazement. My two friends also stopped because I had pointed to the sky. The younger one of the two brothers said excitedly, "Flying saucers!" I turned round to him and said, "I don't think flying saucers exist". In the next sixty seconds I changed my mind, for clearly visible in the blue skies were three very large discs, apparently metallic, gleaming in the daylight, forming a triangular pattern and moving very slowly.
Then I went through a process of wanting to eliminate all possible phenomena to explain away this sighting - planets, moon, birds, aeroplanes, sun and weather balloons. So I made a note of the direction in which the wind was moving the clouds and realised that these three discs seemed as though they were bolted together by sturdy, invisible rods and were moving solidly, traversing against the wind. As my theory about weather balloons faded into dust it dawned on me that we were indeed witnessing apparently metallic, flying discs - the proverbial "flying saucers". I could not understand how such large objects stayed aloft or how they maintained the triangular formation. They had no wings, appendages for engines or seemingly any outward motive power. I got the impression of great prowess and exactitude. I was thrilled. I felt a Holy Presence. It is as if the flying discs were just not spacecraft, they were holy vehicles. There was no sound. I was familiar with civil aircraft flying in and out of Heathrow airport in west London.

So astounded was I by this first shock of the sighting, that I next did something that resulted in the second shock of the day. I formulated a question in my mind and projected it at the trio of saucers. Then arrived the second shock of the day! I received an answer to my question, direct

into my mind. It was not a voice outside of my head but a reply to my question which travelled right into my brain.
In less than a minute, on this weekday morning, my concept of reality was totally shattered. Everything that I had heard from scientists about the existence of extra-terrestrial life was proven wrong. If any scientist said, "Telepathy does not exist", from now on I would not believe them because my own, personal experience said otherwise. To this day I marvel that a teenage boy like myself could have asked such a profound question and received a reply, so deep and all encompassing. Not that I fully understood the reply at the time. It was much later that part of the mysterious reply made any sense to me.

The day three flying saucers came to Wimbledon
In 1964, I was in the lower sixth form, studying mathematics and physics. I was no day dreamer or fantasist. Up until this time, I had thought that flying saucers did not exist but my experience forced me to change my mind. I would have been a fool to deny this outstanding sighting. I had said to my younger friend, "I do not think flying saucers exist". I did not say, "Flying saucers do not exist" as though it were a universal truth. I said, *"I do not think.........".* In other words I was professing ignorance about a subject I knew nothing about at the time. At that time I sincerely believed flying saucers do not exist.

The three of us watched the trio of discs moving towards a bank of cloud. The cloud was moving with the wind but the objects were not, thus negating my earlier theory of weather balloons. The saucers moved into the cloud but did not come out the other side. All three of us were now excited. We waited for the triangular pattern to emerge out of the bank of cloud but they did not do so. We wanted to see where they were going next but it seemed that they were swallowed up by the "cloud". As a result of waiting for them to show themselves again, we were late to school that morning. That was a personal embarrassment to me as I was a sub-prefect at the school and one of my duties was to note down the names of pupils who were late! I was always punctual - except on this fateful day.

I recall that because I was late to school, I went straight to my classroom and bypassed the daily service which usually included a pep talk from the headmaster. My school was at that time known as the Wimbledon County Boys Secondary School. I avoided any disturbance to the morning service by going directly to the sixth-form classroom where I found another student who had also just arrived late. I blurted out to him, a boy by the name of Martin Judd, that I had "just seen three flying saucers". He burst out laughing and retorted, "Don't be silly. Flying saucers don't exist". I felt immediately deflated. His reaction was not one of curiosity but a rigid denial, as though he *knew* for certain.

Later that morning, I spoke to another pupil, David Morgan, who was a lot more thoughtful and enquiring. David even asked me to sketch the objects and was curious about their shape, colour, speed and whether they emitted any sound. He wanted to know if they made any engine noise. **The 'saucers' were totally silent.** From the clouds in the sky we surmised that the three objects must have been at an altitude of between 1,000 and 2,000 feet. From the apparent angle subtended by the objects, I calculated that each disc was about 70 feet in diameter. I was studying mathematics and physics, so this was an easy task for me to do. I went to the local library after that - to learn more about a subject I knew very little about. Since that time, through the years I have read dozens and dozens of books about 'unidentified flying objects' but I learnt a great deal from that one personal experience, which was ***real and undeniable***.

London University undergraduate

Two years later I was a student at Imperial College, part of the University of London, when another extraordinary happening in my life took place. One Friday afternoon, just as I was about to enter a lecture theatre, I stopped and turned to look at someone sat on a nearby bench, reading a book. I suddenly walked up to him, following an inner urge and said, **"I must read that book".** I had no idea what the book was about, who the author was or even who this young man was. He smiled and said, "I am reading the book now, why don't you see me on Monday?" I asked him his name. It was Robert S. and it turned out that he was another student at the college whom I had not met until now. On Monday he handed me the book. It was written by Dr. George King and entitled, **"The Nine Freedoms"**. *At the time I had never heard of George King or the organisation that he had founded, namely The Aetherius Society.* I had never heard of this book nor did I know what the subject matter was. *All I knew was that I had to read the book.* It was as if my higher consciousness had judged a book by its vibrations, not its cover. I took it home and read it in one sitting through the night, so absorbing was it to me. So outstanding were the claims made in the book that I determined to find out more.

The book, "The Nine Freedoms" was my amazing introduction to the Aetherius Society and its teachings. Robert S. told me that there was an Aetherius Society group running at Imperial College and I could find out more if I attended their meetings. So I went along to two weekly meetings and listened to two tape-recorded lectures given by Dr. George King.

The first one was called **"The Seven Dimensions"** and the other one was titled **"The Four Aspects of Creation."** I was spellbound by the knowledge disseminated by Dr. King in both these lectures. They went far beyond the knowledge I was acquiring on my engineering course at Imperial College. Then I asked one of the other students, by the name of Anthony Buckland whether the Aetherius Society had a "God concept"? He handed me a copy of **"The Twelve Blessings"** and said, "Study the Twelfth Blessing". Then he said to me, "The Society will be holding a special meeting this Friday, why don't you go along to their London Headquarters in Fulham Road?" So I did.

July 8th

Little did I realise at the time that it was July 8th 1966, my second anniversary of the sighting of three discs over Wimbledon. The meeting on 8th July 1966 was the most inspiring spiritual service that I had ever attended. By that time I had been inside Buddhist temples, Christian churches, an Islamic mosque, a Sikh gurdwara and Hindu mandirs - but this meeting was literally **"out of this world"**.

On the display, at 757 Fulham Road, was another book titled, **"The Day The Gods Came"** also written by the Founder and President of the Society. Beneath the title it said, *"On July 8th, 1964 the greatest event in the history of the world took place."* I was shocked! I recalled that was the day I had my splendid sighting together with my two friends, RS (not to be confused with Robert S. who I met later at Imperial College) and his younger brother PS. Later in the evening, I was chatting with one of the staff members of the Aetherius Society, a Mr. Tom Curtis and he told me that on 8th July 1964, there had been many 'flying saucers' around Earth and this was their second Commemoration of the day which the Aetherius Society regards *as the most important day in their calendar*. Apparently we three schoolboys had sighted three of these extra-terrestrial craft without premonition.

By my own logic now, as a fairly reasonable person, I was beholden to investigate further the teachings and workings of the Aetherius Society. The turn of events, strange and inexplicable as they were, had brought me to Aetherius House in south-west London on 8th July 1966. Thus started a many-decades investigation into the Aetherius Society, which included a 3-month stay at the headquarters of the Society in Los Angeles in California during the summer of 1968, at which time I was able to observe Dr. George King and his close staff at work, disseminating an important message to the whole world.

A realistic rendering of the 3 flying disks seen on 8th July 1964. Artwork by Frank Warren

This unexpected introduction to the Aetherius Society, whilst I was an undergraduate student at Imperial College in London, prompted me to study in detail some of the "Cosmic Transmissions" that George King had stated had been delivered through him, whilst he was in a self-induced, Yogic, Samadhic trance and which had been recorded on magnetic tape. In those days, the Aetherius Society made its recordings on quarter-inch, reel-to-reel tapes; many years later converted to cassette tapes as technological progress was made in sound and music archiving.

Dr. George King and I met in Los Angeles in the summer of 1968 and I had the opportunity to ask him many questions about his claims of contact with extraterrestrial beings. Dr. King had demonstrated live on BBC his ability to enter a yogic Samadhic trance state to receive a communication. There is a recording of this programme called "Lifeline", made in May, 1959, on a BBC website, link below:

http://www.bbc.co.uk/blogs/adamcurtis/entries/f0960ae2-b142-3d97-8eef-aee310388568?postId=113798748&initial_page_size=20

The demonstration was conducted in front of two sceptical psychologists and an astronomer - who, if they initially thought that they might be speaking with a deluded 'nutcase', must have been very shocked to hear a highly articulate gentleman present his case in a logical and sanguine manner. George King was the 'king of contactees' on that day in May, 1959.

THE TRICK MEMO

In September 1968, I was waiting for a flight back to New York, at Los Angeles (LAX) International airport. I was breaking journey between Los Angeles and New York to visit my sister in Albany, New York state before catching a flight back to the UK.

I noticed that the bookstalls displayed prominently a paperback called, **"UFOs? YES!"** The subtitle of this book was intriguing, to say the least: "WHERE THE CONDON COMMITTEE WENT WRONG".

After spending three months at the headquarters of the Aetherius Society in Los Angeles, I was on my way back to England to start a course at the University of Hull in Yorkshire in October 1968. I was aware that the University of Colorado had been doing a research project to study reports of Unidentified Flying Objects (UFO), under the directorship of physicist Dr. Edward Condon. The subtitle of the book "UFOs? YES!" was an obvious reference to Dr. Condon's committee, which was about to issue its long-awaited report that had been commissioned by the US Air Force in 1966.

My interest in "flying saucers", or UFOs - as the Air Force Project Bluebook had officially designated them in March 1952 – had started with a personal sighting of three "flying disks" on July 8th, 1964. After witnessing these three objects on my way to school, at about 8.50 am, on a sunny day, I started to study the subject by taking a greater interest in reports about unusual objects seen in the sky, throughout the world. My fascination with what I had seen with my own eyes, led me to read several books about 'flying saucers', including purported meetings with alleged "space people". I maintained a healthy attitude towards these claims, neither dismissing them out of hand, nor uncritically believing every word I read.

In 1965, I had embarked on an engineering course at London University. It was here that I came across a remarkable book in a fairly mysterious manner. The book, called "THE NINE FREEDOMS" was written by Dr. George King, Founder and President of the Aetherius Society. This deeply philosophical book opened my eyes to the serious possibility of contact with extraterrestrial intelligence. And that is why I had visited Los Angeles, keen to meet with and talk to a prominent 'flying saucer' "contactee", Dr.George King, who had actually founded the Aetherius Society in England in 1955.

I wish to make it clear that at the time of my sighting on 8th July 1964, I had not heard of Dr. George King, or the Aetherius Society.

The term contactee can be applied to anyone who claims that they have received some kind of contact from space intelligences. By that definition, I have to declare that I too am a 'contactee'. However, Dr. Goerge King stood head and shoulders above all other contactees that I have investigated. More about Dr. George King later……..

To come back to the opening paperback, "UFOs? YES!", the book written by Dr. David R. Saunders and R. Roger Harkins, was an eye-opener about the way that the Condon Committee had conducted its supposed scientific study of UFOs. When the Condon committee eventually produced its report, "Scientific Study of Unidentified Flying Objects", many perceived it as a whitewash but I was determined, one day, to do a thorough study of this massive tome, which was over 900 pages long and had taken over 3 years to publish.

The Conclusions and Recommendations, right at the front of the Condon Report, were somewhat ambivalent and not unduly impressive. I was particularly perturbed by this remark by Dr. Edward U. Condon: **"Careful consideration of the record as it is available to us leads us to conclude that further extensive study of UFOs probably cannot be justified in the expectation that science will be advanced thereby".**

Apart from the fact that this remark did not distinguish between UFOs and *reports of sightings of UFOs*, it stifled open thought and debate about the subject. It did not address the indisputable fact that within the Condon Report itself, over thirty-three percent of the cases that the University of Colorado studied could not be explained. This astonishing fact is a counter to Condon's claim that science might not be advanced thereby. It is by studying the inexplicable deeper, that advances in science, philosophy and general knowledge have taken place throughout the centuries. Having just spent three months at the headquarters of the Aetherius Society, I was convinced, more than ever before, that the claims made by Dr. George King of his contact with extraterrestrial intelligence deserved careful, scientific scrutiny, worthy even of a university's academic department.

UFOs Yes!

The book, "UFOs? YES!" was certainly an antidote to such a negative conclusion as in Condon's report. The fact that it had just been published in September 1968, some weeks before Condon's report came out was indicative of the public interest in this subject. It was evident that the study at the University of Colorado had been marred by dissension and controversy during its progress. As a matter of fact, David Saunders had been sacked by Edward Condon, from the study committee because he had been instrumental in revealing an internal memo to a journalist and other scientists. This shocking memo had been written by the Project's co-ordinator and was undoubtedly proof, that right from the start, the Condon Committee was being driven in a negative direction. This insightful memo which had lain in a filing cabinet deserves a careful analysis here. Written by Robert Low on 9 August 1966, it establishes the proposed direction that the study was to take:

"Our study would be conducted almost exclusively by nonbelievers who, although they couldn't possibly *prove* a negative result, could and probably would add an impressive body of evidence that there is no reality to the observations.
The trick would be, I think, to describe the project so that, to the public, it would appear a totally objective study but, to the scientific community, would present the image of a group of nonbelievers trying their best to be objective but having an almost zero expectation of finding a saucer.
One way to do this would be to stress investigation, not of the physical phenomena, but rather of the people who do the observing – the psychology and sociology of persons and groups who report seeing UFOs. If the emphasis were put here, rather than on examination of the old question of the physical reality of the saucer, I think the scientific community would quickly get the message".

Robert Low, Condon Committee Coordinator,
9 August 1966.

A LOW BLOW

What is astounding about Robert Low's memorandum is its gall. He makes no bones about the fact that he wanted the University of Colorado project to present to the scientific community the image "**that there is no reality to the observations**".

Having witnessed three disks on my way to school on the 8th July 1964, I *knew* of the reality of the phenomenon. I started to be concerned that what many people had believed - that there was a conspiracy to cover-up the reality of the saucers - may well be true. This disturbed me because I had all along believed in the purity of scientific research, convinced that if science stuck with its principles of 'seeking the truth'; it would ultimately find the truth about 'flying saucers'. But here was disturbing evidence that some people had already made up their minds, even before official investigations had started. That did not sound like science to me.

The uncritical belief that some people displayed in many of the claims made about extraterrestrial contact also concerned me. I felt that there was a need for an objective analysis, on scientific grounds. Which is why the *contents* of the Condon Report were, in part, of much interest to me, even if the Conclusions and Summary, as written by Dr. Edward Condon, were somewhat negative. For a study to be unable to explain over 30 percent of cases studied was quite astonishing! The US Air Force had, as its investigations proceeded from the initial Project Sign, to Project Grudge and then to Project Bluebook, taken much care to keep the number of 'unidentifieds' in its files, down to a few percent. Sometimes, the "books had been cooked" to retain a very low percentage, such as 3 or 4 percent on an annual basis. This must have been a deliberate policy to show that efforts were being made to try and explain every sighting report but some had insufficient information to draw firm conclusions.

Low also clearly made a distinction between what he called non-believers and believers. Elsewhere in this memo, Robert Low states, "**Believers, in other words, remain outcasts**". I do not think that a scientific study should be based on a distinction between believers and non-believers. A scientific study should be based on all available evidence and the conclusions should be drawn based on the results of the study. Science should travel where the evidence leads, regardless of whether anticipations are met or not met.

Robert Low was being disingenuous in wanting to move the investigation away from the *physical phenomenon* to a study of the people who do the observing. He categorically stated in his notorious memo,
"If the emphasis were put here……"

When Project Bluebook was finally closed down by the US Air Force, 701 reports of sightings remained unexplained!

There should be an intensive study of people who claim contact with ETI (extraterrestrial intelligence) as well as a study of people who observe and report sightings of UFOs. The latter probably happen to be in the right place at the right time and wish to make sense of what they have just observed. Having spoken to many witnesses, I realise that people are genuinely puzzled by their encounters and would like official statements about the reality of the phenomena observed. People like to know what it is that they have seen, in most cases - quite unexpectedly.

On the other hand, persons who claim contact fall into a different category. Today, there is a distinction between "contactee" and "abductee". It is the "contactees" that are of paramount importance. Their claims are either true or not and the difference needs to be firmly established. Which was one of the reasons I had travelled to Los Angeles in the summer of 1968, in order to meet with and observe England's primary contactee, Dr. George King, late Founder and President of the Aetherius Society.

PART TWO - THE NUCLEAR CONNECTION

CHAPTER 4

Major Donald Keyhoe and NICAP

The first few books on the subject that I had read since 1964 were written by major Donald Keyhoe, who remained embroiled in a war-of-words with the US Air Force about "flying saucers".

Keyhoe directed the National Investigations Committee on Aerial Phenomena (NICAP). Most of the research papers and investigation reports by NICAP personnel are today archived by Mr. Francis Ridge at:

http://www.nicap.org

The NICAP site has a section called, **"Nuclear Connection Cases".** It is clear that nuclear sites throughout the world have been 'monitored' by UFOs since 1945.

According to declassified FBI and U.S. Air Force documents, the U.S. equivalent of the AWE facility - the Los Alamos Laboratory in New Mexico - was repeatedly monitored by UFOs, as early as December 1948. The NICAP site documents incidents in January and February of 1945 over Hanford Nuclear Reservation. Other U.S. nuclear weapons laboratories under apparent surveillance in the early 1950s included Oak Ridge, Tennessee, and Sandia Laboratory, in Albuquerque, New Mexico. Also documented on the NICAP site are events from several Inter Continental Ballistic Missile (ICBM) sites that were visited by unidentified aerial vehicles.

Cosmic Voice

George King had started a journal in the 1950's, appropriately titled "Cosmic Voice" which printed verbatim the Transmissions which he said had been delivered through him, whilst he was in a Yogic, Samadhic trance state. Quite apart from his three books I had previously mentioned in my narration, I was intrigued by several others which dealt with the dangers of radioactivity and the immorality of atmospheric testing of nuclear weapons, leaving so many of the world's population exposed to radioactive dust clouds encircling our globe.

Russian nuclear accident

One of the transmissions which caught my eye in particular, reported by George King to have been received on 18th April 1958, stated the following:

"Owing to an atomic accident just recently in the USSR, a great amount of radio-activity in the shape of radioactive iodine, strontium 90, radioactive nitrogen and radioactive sodium, have been released into the atmosphere of Terra." (Mars Sector 6)

"All forms of reception from Interplanetary sources will become a little more difficult during the next few weeks because of the foolish actions of Russia. *They have not yet declared to the world as a whole, exactly what happened in one of their atomic research establishments.* **Neither have they declared how many people were killed there. Neither have they declared that they were really frightened by the tremendous release of radio-active material from this particular establishment during the accident........certain damage has already been done to large land and water masses." (Master Aetherius)**

[Extract from Cosmic Voice Issue No. 16 - June/July 1958]

My reaction

I was perturbed when I first read this in 1966. No nation has a right to place their citizens in harm's way. Or was a young man's idealism blinding him to the practical realities of a modern world? We were in a Cold War situation and the precarious peace could be shattered by any nation's unilateral nuclear actions, accidental or deliberate.

Surely we in the West would have had some inkling of such a serious accident? But there had been scant information then, in 1958, in the American or European press, unlike the Chernobyl accident many years later (which occurred on 26th April 1986 and became headline news throughout the world a few days after the horrible event.)

It was not until 1976, *nearly twenty years later*, that the truth about a huge explosion at an atomic site in the Ural mountains, came to light. And it came to light via a Soviet dissident, by the name of Zhores A. Medvedev. He revealed in the science magazine, *"New Scientist"* many facts about the accident in the Ural mountains, near Kyshtym. A book by Medvedev, "NUCLEAR DISASTER IN THE URALS" was published in 1979 after publication of the *New Scientist* article.

In the New Scientist of 4th November 1976, Medvedev wrote in an article entitled: **"Two Decades of Dissidence"**, the following:

"A tragic catastrophe occurred in 1958, which made nuclear physicists extremely sensitive to the radiobiological and genetics issue. The catastrophe itself could have been foreseen. For many years nuclear reactor waste had been buried in a deserted area not more than a few dozen miles from the Urals town of Blagoveshensk. The waste was not buried very deep. Nuclear scientists had often warned about the dangers involved in this primitive method of waste disposal but nobody took their views seriously. The alternative of drowning the containers in the very deep waters of the Pacific or Indian Oceans had been rejected as too expensive and protracted. Dispersing the highly radioactive materials over other parts of the country was also considered unnecessary. The large nuclear industry, concentrated in the Urals, just continued to bury its waste in the same way it had done since the beginning of the atomic race. *Suddenly there was an enormous explosion like a violent volcano.* The nuclear reactions had led to overheating in the underground burial grounds. The explosion poured radioactive dust and materials high up into the sky. It was just the wrong weather for such a tragedy.

Ghastly repercussions

"Strong winds blew the radioactive cloud hundreds of miles away. It was difficult to gauge the extent of the disaster immediately, and no evacuation plan was put into operation right away. Many villages and towns were only ordered to evacuate when the symptoms of radiation sickness were already quite apparent. *Tens of thousands of people were affected, **hundreds dying**, though the real figures have never been made public.* The large area, where the accident happened, is still considered dangerous and is closed to the public. A number of biological stations have been built on the edge of this - the largest gamma field in the world - in order to study the radioactive damage done to plants and animals.

"The irradiated population was distributed over many clinics. But no one really knew how to treat the different stages of radiation sickness, how to measure the radiation dose received by the patient, how to predict what the effects would be both for the patients and their offspring. Radiation genetics and radiology could have provided the answer but neither of them was available. There was no laboratory in the whole of the country which could make a routine investigation of chromosome aberrations - the most evident result of radiation exposure; marrow stocks did not exist; there was no chemical protection against radiation exposure available for immediate distribution.

Lack of preparation

"Many towns and villages where the radioactive level was moderate or high, but not lethal, were not evacuated. The observation medical teams established in them were not well prepared for serious tests. .....
"The nuclear physicists were now well aware of the real dangers of nuclear explosions. They were no longer just an obedient group of experts. Their strong opposition to government policy contributed considerably to the final agreement to end atmospheric tests of nuclear devices."

[New Scientist, published in the UK, 1976]

Thus Dr. Zhores Medvedev, in 1976, brought to the attention of the British scientific community, facts about a nuclear accident which had been reported by George King, Founder of the Aetherius Society, in his journal, "Cosmic Voice" way back in 1958, shortly after the major explosion had happened.

Dr. Medvedev, in a follow-up article in the "New Scientist", on 30th June 1977, **"Facts behind the Soviet nuclear disaster"** wrote:

"In my article **"Two Decades of Dissidence"** (*New Scientist*, vol 72, page 264), I mentioned the occurrence at the end of 1957, or beginning of 1958, of a nuclear disaster in the southern Urals. I described how the disaster had resulted from a sudden explosion involving nuclear waste stored in underground shelters, not far from where the first Soviet military reactors had been built; how strong winds carried a mixture of radioactive products and soil over a large area, probably more than a thousand square miles in size; and how many villages and small towns were not evacuated on time, probably causing the deaths later of several hundred people from radiation sickness."

Dr. Medvedev makes a pointed remark:

"I was unaware at the time that this nuclear disaster was absolutely unknown to Western experts and my *New Scientist* article created an unexpected sensation. Reports about this 20-year-old nuclear disaster appeared in almost all the major newspapers. At the same time, some

Western nuclear experts, including the chairman of the United Kingdom Atomic Energy Authority, Sir John Hill, tried to dismiss my story as "science-fiction", "rubbish" or a "figment of the imagination".

Dr. Medvedev gave further details about radioactive materials which is worth reading carefully at this juncture:

"Different kinds of nuclear accidents release different kinds of radioactive products into the environment. If *reactor nuclear waste* is scattered from a storage area the result will be quite specific.

"The numerous short-lived radioactive isotopes, with very intense gamma and beta radiation, will already have disappeared during the storage period. Only long-lived isotopes, which constitute about 5 to 6 per cent of the initial radioactivity, remain dangerous after the first two to three months.

"Radioactive strontium-90 and caesium-137 are the most important of these. Both have half-lives of about 30 years. *Caesium-137, as an isotope with gamma radiation, is more dangerous for external irradiation.* However, it is less cumulative and because it is more soluble and is not fixed permanently in biological structures, it disappears more rapidly from animals and the soil.

"Strontium-90 is a close analogue of calcium and is able to substitute for calcium in both bones and soil. Since calcium forms parts of permanent body structure, this means that strontium-90 can be fixed in animals for many years, while it may remain for hundreds of years in the soil. *This is why strontium-90, which emits beta radiationis considered the most dangerous product from nuclear bomb tests and the nuclear industry."*

==

The fact that Dr.George King had first published details about the accident in the Urals in April 1958, should give pause for thought by sceptics, about his claim to have received vital information from extraterrestrial sources. Many scientists who are sceptical about claims of UFO contact, should now consider:

"What were the lines of communication that Dr. George King had, that allowed him to be a primary conduit for knowledge of this level?"

Often, sceptical persons have asked: "What useful knowledge have "alleged" extraterrestrial contacts produced?" Here is a remarkable case in point.

Dr. Medvedev had written - as a subtitle to his second article in the *New Scientist* -
"When the story first came to light last year (1976), Western nuclear experts were sceptical that a large accident, involving nuclear waste materials, could have occurred in the south Urals in **late 1957 or early 1958.** However, *published* Soviet research into the effect of radioactivity on plants and animals *confirms that a nuclear disaster did contaminate hundreds of square miles of the region."*

Dr. Medvedev further elaborated:

"If the nuclear disaster in the Urals really caused the contamination of hundreds or thousands of square miles of territory, this area must still be polluted today (i.e in 1977) - heavily by strontium-90 and partly by caesium-137.
"The soil, soil animals, plants, insects, mammals, lakes, fish and all other forms of life in this area would still contain significant amounts of strontium-90 and caesium-137. The random distribution of radioactive isotopes during an accident of this type would cause the isotope concentration level to vary enormously from place to place. In many areas the external and internal radiation would seriously threaten the life of many species -- increasing their mutation load and mortality and inducing many other changes. The extremely large contaminated area would also create a unique community of animals and plants, where genetic, population, botanical, zoological and limnological research into the influence of radioactive contamination could be studied in its natural conditions."

This raises another important question - "Why were Western scientists so sceptical about such an accident happening?" When we revisit the comments made by the then Chairman of the UK Atomic Energy Authority, perhaps fear about public reaction to the entire nuclear industry may have played a part in such knee-jerk reactions.

Medvedev tackled the irrational scepticism in his second article:

"Critics of my story can obviously ask why then did Soviet scientists miss this chance to study the unique radiobiological and genetic problems, which this enormous (certainly the largest in the world) radioactive environment provided for long-term study?"

Dr. Zhores Medvedev answered his own question with inescapable conclusions:

"The answer is very simple - the Soviet scientists *did not miss this chance.* More than 100 works on the effect of strontium-90 and caesium-137 in natural plant and animal populations has been published since 1958.

"In most of these publications, *neither the cause nor the geographical location of the contaminated area are indicated.* **This is the unavoidable price of censorship.** However, the specific composition of the plants and animals, the climate, soil types and many other indicators leads to the inevitable conclusion that *it lies in the south Urals.* (In one publication, the Cheliabinsk region is actually mentioned - a censorship slip.)"

Medvedev penned another astute insight:

"The terms of observation -- 10 years in 1968, 11 in 1969, 14 in 1971 and so on -- reveal the *approximate date* of the original accident. Finally, the scale of the research (especially with mammals, birds and fish) indicates clearly that rather heavy radioactive contamination covered hundreds of square miles of an area *containing several large lakes."*

The furore caused by Medvedev's articles in the *New Scientist* did eventually lead to a public announcement by the Soviet Union about a catastrophic nuclear accident in 1957 and/or 1958. The revelation included some obfuscation of facts, muddled with the possibility of *two major accidents* having happened within 6 months of each other.
One accident, said to have occurred in 1957 was said to have caused no casualties but widespread dispersal of radioactive elements. The second in 1958 was not clearly defined by date.

===

I had written two articles for the Sri Lanka UFO Register, trying to clarify the issue, which are reproduced here.

HOW AETHERIUS BROKE THE NEWS ABOUT RUSSIA'S NUCLEAR TRAGEDY

When the Aetherius Society first revealed the facts about Russia's nuclear accident in the Ural mountains, in the June/July 1958 Issue of "Cosmic Voice", there was not even a ripple in the Western Press.

Yet, in 1976, eighteen years later, when Soviet biochemist - dissident Dr. Zhores Medvedev *proved* that the accident had occurred and details about its after-effects were available in technical journals freely accessible in a London library, there was commotion in the British Press; during which time the Chairman of the UK Atomic Energy Authority got himself deeply embroiled in the controversy.

The science journal *'New Scientist'*, which thought it had been the first to bring Medvedev's stunning news to the West, had to admit that it had been **"Scooped By A UFO"**! The reference in the *New Scientist* to an unidentified flying object was an allusion to the source of knowledge claimed by the Founder and President of the Aetherius Society, Dr. George King, who has, since 1954, stated that he is capable of telepathic communication with Cosmic Intelligences, utilising a Yogic, Samadhic trance-state, during which verbal statements given through him are tape-recorded live. (See the *New Scientist*, Volume 78, No. 1100, April 1978)

George King demonstrated this unique ability on a BBC TV programme called "Lifeline" on 21st May, 1959.

The nuclear disaster was shown to have happened a thousand miles east of Moscow, between Chelyabinsk and Sverdlovsk. It turned two massive lakes into radioactive cesspits. An area hundreds of square miles had been turned into a nuclear wasteland. There is no doubt whatsoever that the Soviet authorities withheld the facts about the accident in 1958.

In 1977, Sir John Hill, Chairman of the UK Atomic Energy Authority, said he was not aware of the accident having taken place, although he challenged details about Medevedev's revelation. This caused Dr. Medvedev to retort:

"John Hill's attitude was one of arrogance, an insult. None of your scientists asked me how I knew of the explosion." (See THE DAILY EXPRESS, 1st July 1977. Interview by Geoffrey Levy: "Don't Let Britain Become The World's Nuclear Cemetry.")

More to the point, none of the scientists or journalists bothered to investigate how the Aetherius Society came to know of the explosion in

1958 and published the news eighteen years before the *New Scientist* thought it was first on the news-stand with its alleged scoop.

The explosion, near Kyshtym, had killed many people, endangered many more lives, turned villages into graveyards and produced grotesque mutation in animal and plant life for many generations after.

The disturbing aspect of the tragedy is why, if the CIA and other Western intelligence agencies had been aware of the accident shortly after, did they not leak it to the Western press? Proceedings under the Freedom of Information Act indicate that the CIA did know about the nuclear accident in the Urals when it happened, despite Sir John Hill's professed ignorance about the explosion. What were Western governments trying to cover?

They usually seize with relish every opportunity they get, to embarrass the Soviet Union - why not that time? Was there fear of public reaction in the West to the dangers of atomic experimentation, the nuclear power industry and its concomitant waste-disposal dilemma? It seems that the "Three Mile Island" accident in the USA was tiny in comparison with Russia's nuclear tragedy.

ITV's "World In Action" programme of 7th November 1977, delved a long way into uncovering what had happened at the time of the accident. Interviews with Russian emigres in Denmark, Japan and Israel indicated that hospital wards in the area had been full of people injured by the nuclear blast, which had occurred in a dump and that thousands may have eventually died as a direct result. The flora and the fauna had been seriously affected by the ecological disturbance.

Dr. Medvedev had uncovered over a hundred scientific papers published by Soviet scientists who had been allowed to study the aftermath later - when blame for the disaster could be placed on the authorities appointed by Nikita Kruschev. Neither ITV, nor any of the British newspapers in 1977 acknowledged a single word of reference to the Aetherius Society journal *"Cosmic Voice"* or its editor - Sir George King. Had Fleet Street lost its sense of fairness and justice towards a British pioneer?

NOTES AND REFERENCES

(1) <u>COSMIC VOICE</u> - Issue No. 16, June/July 1958. Published by the Aetherius Society, Fulham Road, London, SW6 5UU.
Cosmic Transmissions delivered by Mars Sector 6 and Master Aetherius on 18th April 1958 at 10.00pm. The editorial in this issue of *Cosmic Voice* by George King, Founder and President of the Aetherius Society, had this to say to the Kremlin:
"STOP ALL ATOMIC EXPERIMENTATION IMMEDIATELY. GIVE THE FULL FACTS REGARDING THIS ACCIDENT TO THE REST OF THE WORLD."
As far as is known at that time, no other political, scientific, news or religious chronicle or journal, that was freely accessible to the public, carried any news about this nuclear disaster in the Urals.

(2) <u>NEW SCIENTIST</u> - Volume 72, page 264, 11th November 1976.
This science journal wrongly thought that they were the first to break this news in an article by Dr. Zhores Medvedev, titled: **"Two Decades of Dissidence"**.

(3) <u>PRESS RELEASE</u> - by the Aetherius Society, 7th November 1976.
This press release reprinted the whole text of the two Cosmic Transmissions by Mars Sector 6 and Aetherius. In the press release, Dr. George King stated:
"The statement by Dr. Medvedev proves the authenticity of my sources. I invite scientists to study the other Transmissions from the Cosmic Masters which deal in great detail with the dangers of atomic experimentation and with the whole aspect of metaphysics."

(4) <u>THE GUARDIAN (UK)</u> - 30th June 1977. **"Nuclear Disaster Proved"**.
In an article by Alec Hartley, the Guardian newspaper referred to the Russian science journal "Atmoniya Energiya", which in 1966 published the results of tests in two contaminated lakes, 11.3 and 4.5 square kilometers in area respectively.
The Guardian stated that research uncovered by Zhores Medvedev showed the effects of excessive exposure to highly radioactive Strontium 90 and Caesium-137. Although these research papers had been strictly censored, one of them contained a slip and mentioned Chelyabinsk as the area of contamination.

(5) <u>DAILY EXPRESS (UK)</u> - 1st July 1977. **"Don't Let Britain Become The World's Nuclear Cemetry"**. Interview by Geoffrey Levy. This interview of Medvedev directly by the Daily Express was probably the

strongest warning in the popular press at the time against all the inherent dangers of the whole atomic process. Part of the article said:

"**What it shows is that either our nuclear scientists are not very well informed, or that particular care is being taken in certain areas to keep us, the public, ignorant.**"

This statement was in regard to John Hill's professed ignorance about the accident. The article continues:

"**One of these must be true. Neither provides much comfort. The explosion (said to be a conventional blast, probably caused by overheated rainwater that blew open a nuclear waste coffin) took place almost 20 years ago.**

"**It turned a region as big as an English county into a nuclear wilderness. Villages there are now deserted, crops and cattle gone, the water undrinkable. The people have been moved and may not be able to return for generations.**"

During his interview, Medvedev gave a stern warning to the UK:

"**I tell you, Britain could well become the nuclear cemetery of the world. And the more you accept it, the more will come. A chain reaction.**"

He continued:

"**Many areas of nuclear research are covered by secrecy - they have to be - and scientists in these fields are not willing to disclose things. They do not like public scrutiny. That is okay when their work is military but even when it is for peaceful uses, they still don't like the public to know everything. That is wrong. So people do not trust scientists.**"

(6) THE SUN (UK) - 7th November 1977. **"A Tragedy They Hid For 20 Years".** This article on their TV page coincided with the ITV programme to be broadcast that same night, in the series "WORLD IN ACTION".

(7) NEW SCIENTIST - 27th April 1978. **"Scooped By A UFO",** in the Feedback Section, page 241. Reluctantly, six months later, the New Scientist admitted that the Aetherius Society and its journal Cosmic Voice had beaten them to it - by about 18 years!

(8) PRESS RELEASE - by the Aetherius Society:
"UFO Contact Genuine", 1st March 1986. This release reiterated the 1958 information received from Aetherius as well as an earlier Transmission received in October 1957 about the Windscale blunder - an accident at a British nuclear facility, now renamed "Sellafield".

The above article was published in the Sri Lanka UFO Register (Kalpa-Nava) in 1986, Issue No. 10.

As the editor of the journal at the time, I had some comments to make as well - **EDITOR'S COMMENTS:**
   "Shocking as it may seem, neither Fleet Street journalists and editors, nor the Independent TV (ITV) programme "World In Action" of 7th November 1977, had the decency to acknowledge that the Aetherius Society had been first with the news of Russia's nuclear tragedy of 1958 just a short time after it had happened.
   Full credit should have gone to the editor of *Cosmic Voice*, Dr. George King, Founder and President of the Aetherius Society, for his courage in having published the news just a matter of weeks after the tragic explosion in March, 1958 but even more symbolic, the source of his first-hand information should have been accredited by both journalists and politicians - namely the Cosmic Transmissions delivered through George King (whilst he was in a Yogic, Samadhic trance) by Aetherius and Mars Sector 6.
   No longer can any well-versed UFO researcher sit on the ET fence, pretending that UFO contactees have never given information or data which can be verified. UFO researchers do not have to go to Mars or Venus to check that Dr. George King published details about the Soviet disaster of 1958 (and the earlier news about the Windscale/Sellafield blunder of 1957), shortly after each terrible event. Publications like *Cosmic Voice* were registered at the British Library as part and parcel of the publication process and could be checked by any diligent researcher, never mind an experienced UFO researcher who is looking at the phenomenon of unidentified aerial vehicles operating freely in our airspace. These objects seem to appear beneath radar coverage and can make themselves invisible, apparently at the 'push of a button'. Any blatant violation of our airspace should be of deep interest to our military and government. Parliament needs to conduct its own investigations, particularly those with security aspects."

==

Dr. George King told me that in 1957, after he received a Transmission entitled: **"You Are Responsible"** from Cosmic sources, he sent a printed copy of that speech to *every Member of Parliament by registered post.* He also told me that a Cosmic Transmission given through him about **"Radioactivity And Cancer"** was sent by special courier to His Royal Highness, the Duke of Edinburgh at Buckingham Palace.

Press release by the Aetherius Society - 7th November 1976

Press Release

Release: Immediate

RUSSIAN ATOMIC ACCIDENT REVEALED 18 YEARS AGO BY MEDIUM

Los Angeles, November 7, 1976 --- The Russian atomic accident at Blagoveshensk in the Ural Mountains which has been disclosed by exiled Soviet scientist, Zhores Medvedev in London, was revealed just after it happened 18 years ago by Cosmic sources through the Mediumship of Sir George King. In answer to requests from the British Broadcasting Corporation and other news media, Sir George, an English-born Master of Yoga and Occult Science, made this statement today at the Los Angeles Headquarters of The Aetherius Society, the International Metaphysical Order of which he is Founder/President.

"On April 18th, 1958 at 10.00 p.m., I went into a positive Yogic trance state known as Samadhi. While I was in that state, Cosmic Masters from other Planets in this Solar System, during the course of a lengthy communication, revealed that a serious nuclear accident had taken place in Russia in which hundreds of lives were lost and thousands more injured.

"It was also revealed that Divine Intervention had taken place, through the agency of what is commonly termed "Flying Saucers" to clean up the horrible mess created by this disaster in the atmosphere, thereby saving a further 17 million lives.

"This statement was published in the June/July, 1958 Issue No. 16 of a magazine called "Cosmic Voice" which, at that time, was published by The Aetherius Society under my editorship. It later appeared in my book "You Are Responsible!", published in May, 1961. Both these publications have had a worldwide distribution. Because of Russia's secrecy, there has been no official confirmation until now.

"The statement by Mr. Medvedev proves the authenticity of my sources. I invite scientists to study the other Transmissions from the Cosmic Masters which deal in great detail with the dangers of atomic experimentation and with the whole aspect of Metaphysics."

...../2

..../2

Following is a text of the excerpts from the Transmission of April 18th, 1958 published in "Cosmic Voice", Issue No. 16, June/July, 1958:

> MARS SECTOR 6: "Owing to an atomic accident just recently in the U.S.S.R., a great amount of radio-activity in the shape of radio-active iodine, strontium 90, radio-active nitrogen and radio-active sodium, have been released into the atmosphere of Terra. (Note 1).
>
> "This Transmission came from Mars Sector 6".
>
> THE MASTER AETHERIUS: "All forms of reception from Interplanetary sources will become a little more difficult during the next few weeks because of the foolish actions of Russia. They have not yet declared to the world as a whole, exactly what happened in one of their atomic research establishments. Neither have they declared how many people were killed there. Neither have they declared that they were really frightened by the tremendous release of radio-active materials from this particular establishment during the accident.
>
> "Because this accident took place, we will most certainly have to use a tremendous amount of energy, which should be used in a very different way. We should not really have to expend this amount of energy clearing away dangerous radio-active clouds from the atmosphere of Terra. However, because of Divine Intervention, we are able to use enough energy in this direction to save about 17,000,000 lives, which otherwise would have been forced to vacate their physical bodies.
>
> "Such were the far-reaching repercussions from this accident that we were given permission by the Lords of Karma to intervene! However, although we are at the moment intervening on behalf of Terra, in this direction, certain damage has already been done to large land and water masses!"

Note 1: Terra is the name used for the Planet Earth.

 - ends -

For further information, please contact: Dr. Richard Lawrence,
European Headquarters Secretary

or: Mr. Tony Perrott,
Public Relations Officer
01-736 4187

Issued by: The Aetherius Society, 757 Fulham Road, London SW6 5UU.

THE TRUTH EMERGES

The Freedom of Information Act has been a boon for those trying to pry out state secrets. On 26th November 1977, one year after Medvedev's scientific report and eleven years before the Chernobyl disaster, the New York times published a story titled:

C.I.A. Papers Released to Nader, Tell of 2 Soviet Nuclear Accidents
WASHINGTON, November 25, 1977 – The Central Intelligence Agency has made public 14 documents that describe two apparently separate nuclear accidents in the Soviet Union, one of which reportedly took the lives of hundreds of people.
The documents, made public, in response to a Freedom of Information Act request by an antinuclear group established by Ralph Nader, appear to confirm a report of two nuclear accidents in the Soviet Union made public a year ago by Dr. Zhores A. Medvedev, an exiled Soviet scientist.

One of the C.I.A. documents, however said it was possible that reports and memos of the nuclear accident may have been prompted by a top-secret test in which the Soviet Union allegedly exploded a 20-megaton device in the air over a mock village populated with goats and sheep, to test the hazards of such an explosion.
Though most of the documents were anecdotal in form and considerable information had been deleted from them, it appeared that the two accidents occurred at a vast nuclear facility near the city of Kyshtym on the eastern slope of the Ural Mountains between 1958 and 1961. One of the reports, dated March 25 1977, quoted an unnamed source as telling the CIA that he had been told "hundreds of people perished and the area became and will remain radioactive for many years."

Affected Region Is Described
The source said that in 1961 he had visited the "strange, uninhabited and unfarmed area" where the accident reportedly had occurred. He described the region this way: "Highway signs along the way warned drivers not to stop for the next 20 to 30 kilometers because of radiation. The land was empty, there were no villages, no towns, no people, no cultivated land, only the chimneys of destroyed houses remained." Thirty kilometres would equal about 20 miles.
A former Soviet physicist, Leo Tumerman, who emigrated to Israel in 1972, described seeing virtually the same scene of desolation on an auto trip that he took through the Kyshtym area, in an account that appeared in the 9th December 1976 issue of the New York times. In it, Dr. Tumerman

said he had been informed that he had passed through the site of the "Kyshtym catastrophe" named for a town in the vicinity and that a nuclear disaster a few years earlier had killed and injured many hundreds of people. He said he thought the year of the explosion was in the late 1950's.

A second report dated 23rd May 1958, painted a portrait of a less serious nuclear accident. "Various Soviet employees and visitors to the Brussels fair have stated independently but consistently that the occurrence of an accidental atomic explosion during the spring of 1958 was widely known throughout the U.S.S.R." The Brussels World's Fair took place in 1958. The 1958 report added: "Rumours are common that many people were killed. However, the general accepted version is that only several score died."

Other reports described a terrible explosion that appeared to have occurred in either 1960 or 1961. The explosion was so great, the report said, that it made the ground and buildings shake. A short time after this explosion, it said, all the leaves on the trees in and around the blast area "were completely covered with a heavy layer of red dust."

Hospital Filled with Victims

This report said that a woman had been in a hospital "at the time of the explosion" and she said that after the blast occurred, she saw many people, brought to this hospital for medical attention. The hospital was eventually filled with victims of the explosion.

Mr. Nader, in an interview questioned the Agency's motives in not making the documents public at an earlier date. "Absent any other reason for withholding information from the public" he said, "One possible motivation could have been the reluctance of the CIA to highlight a nuclear accident in the USSR that could cause concern among people living near nuclear facilities in the united States."

In November 1976, Dr. Medvedev, a dissident biochemist, writing in the British weekly New Scientist, charged that hundreds of people had been killed and thousands suffered radiation sickness in 1958 when atomic wastes buried in the Ural mountains exploded.

A further article written by myself, appeared in the journal of the Sri Lanka UFO Register No. 13.

AETHERIUS SOCIETY VINDICATED - SOVIET UNION ADMITS NUCLEAR ACCIDENT

The Aetherius Society has been vindicated by the Soviet Union's official admission that a nuclear disaster did occur in the Urals in the late 1950's. There were probably two disastrous accidents - one in 1957 and the other in 1958. Details about them have been convoluted and obfuscated.

As reported in *Kalpa-Nava* Issue No. 10 (HOW AETHERIUS BROKE THE NEWS ABOUT RUSSIA'S NUCLEAR TRAGEDY) the Aetherius Society broke the news about a nuclear disaster to the world in April 1958 via its journal *Cosmic Voice*.

It was not until 1977 that the free press of the world reported this news in the West. The bare facts of the matter are as follows:

On the 18th April 1958, the Founder and President of the Aetherius Society, Dr. George King, English-born yogi adept and mystic extraordinaire, tape recorded what he said was a Cosmic Transmission delivered through him by an extraterrestrial intelligence. The full text of this Transmission was published in the Aetherius Society bulletin *Cosmic Voice*, Issue No. 16 - June/July 1958.

This particular Transmission was republished in May 1961 in the book written by Sir George King entitled "You Are Responsible", which has been publicly available ever since. I purchased a copy of this book in 1966 from the headquarters of the Society in Fulham Road, London. It was not until 1977, when the *New Scientist* published vivid details about the accident and its terrible aftermath, uncovered by the Soviet dissident and researcher, Dr. Zhores Medvedev, that the Western press even acknowledged the possibility of a major nuclear disaster happening in the USSR. The press did not credit Dr. George King for his pioneering work. That much was reported in *Kalpa-Nava* in 1986.

The Soviet Union initially denied that such an accident had taken place but after the Chernobyl disaster in 1986 and with the freer flow of information resulting from 'glasnost', *Nucleonics Week* reported in 1988 that the Soviet Union was hinting at the "official" release of further information about the Ural mountains accident.

The official Russian revelation was finally made by the USSR, on the 16th June 1989 by the "Minister for Medium Machine Building", 30 years plus after the tragic accident. The same number of years after the Aetherius Society had broken the news, 13 years after the *New Scientist* article "Two Decades of Dissidence" and 3 years after my short article.

No clear-thinking and fair-minded researcher can fail to be impressed with the vindication of the Aetherius Society about this matter and give due credit to its Founder - Dr. George King.

After all these years, it seems that the nuclear nightmare for residents in the Urals is not over! A newsclipping on Wednesday 22nd November 2017, sixty years later, reported that:
"Russia's meteorological service yesterday confirmed "extremely high" levels of radioactivity over the Ural mountains. France previously said it may have come from a nuclear fuel spill accident."

By now I had been studying the many Transmissions that had been tape recorded by George King and had been published in Cosmic Voice. There had been another, earlier statement, about a nuclear accident in 1957 in the United kingdom.

MARS AND THE WINDSCALE BLUNDER

On October 10th, 1957, an accident took place at the Windscale nuclear plant (now renamed Sellafield) in northern England in Cumbria. This "blunder" was to have far-reaching effects and long-term consequences for the United Kingdom Atomic Energy Authority (UK AEA).
   The accident occured during a routine process of maintenance called the "Wigner release". The immediate cause of the accident was described as the "application, too soon and at too rapid a rate, of a second nuclear heating" to release the "Wigner" energy from graphite rods. This caused the failure of cartridges in the nuclear pile. The pile with the adversely affected cartridges oxidised slowly, leading to a fire in the reactor. Windscale (Sellafield) is a nuclear fuel reprocessing and nuclear decommissioning plant.

   The increased radioactivity resulting from this accident, caused by human blunder, was first detected between 11.00 and 14.00 hours on 10th October 1957. That the accident happened was not a secret.
   By Saturday 12th October, when analysis of the neighbourhood morning milk production was known, the Health Physics Manager at Windscale advised the Works General Manager that the distribution of the milk should be halted.
   Radioactive iodine in the milk, was found to be at a level way above that believed to be a hazard to infants. Deliveries from twelve milk producers, within a two-mile radius of the Windscale plant, were prevented with the co-operation of the milk Marketing Board and the local police.

From midday Thursday to midday Saturday, constituted a period of 48 hours, during which radioactive vapours spewed out of the nuclear plant. Restrictions on the distribution of milk were extended successively until it covered a strip along the coast, a corridor ten miles long and thirty miles wide.

On Tuesday, 29th October 1957, the British Prime Minister, Harold Macmillan stated to the House of Parliament:

"The government are fully aware of the public anxiety that has been caused both generally and locally."

He revealed that the AEA had appointed a Committee of Inquiry consisting of "Eminent scientists with experience of atomic energy, who are unconnected with with the industrial group group of the AEA under whose control Windscale is."

On the same day, 29th October 1957, the Aetherius Society stated that George King had received several Cosmic Transmissions from interplanetary intelligences delivered whilst he was in a self-induced Yogic, Samadhic trance state and had been tape recorded, as was the usual practice.

One of these Transmissions was called: "THE WINDSCALE BLUNDER" and stated to have been given by an Intelligence with the Code Name of Mars Sector 8. The Society published the full text of these Transmissions in its journal *Cosmic Voice*, Issue No. 13 (December / January 1957/1958).

The Aetherius Society maintains that this Transmission was given by a Martian intelligence and a quote from this represents a very serious charge:

"I would like to make it known that your scientists have not , in any way even attempted to give you a true account of the full damage done by the escape of plutonium dust and radioactive iodine and also strontium-90 from Windscale.

"Upon their heads then, does it rest!"

MARS SECTOR 8

(Copyright The Aetherius Society, 1957. Reproduced with acknowledgement to the late Dr. George King)

On the 8th November 1957, the British Prime Minister, stated to the house:

"There is no evidence that this accident has done any significant harm to any person, animal or property."

The statement was made by Harold Macmillan (later the Earl of Stockton, deceased in 1986) based on the report made to him by two Committees of Inquiry, one set up by the UK Atomic Energy Authority and the other set up, on the 29th October 1957, by the Medical Research Council.

It was 26 years later that the official truth emerged!

Headlines in the Daily Express of Friday, 18th February 1983, ran:
"BRITAIN'S A-PLANT VICTIMS - 13 DEATHS FROM WINDSCALE LEAK SAY EXPERTS".
The newspaper article elaborated further:
"Britain's worst nuclear accident may have caused many cases of cancer, an official report revealed last night."
"The total estimated for the first time: 260 cases, 13 of them fatal. They are, or will be, the victims of a raging fire in 1957 at the Windscale reactor in Cumbria, which was producing plutonium for atom bombs."

The report was issued by the National Radiation Protection Board (NRPB) set up in 1970. Since that time, British Nuclear Fuels (BNF), which runs the present Windscale plant for the reprocessing of waste materials has paid out nearly £500,000 (half a million pounds sterling) in compensation to the families of cancer victims among the workers at what has now been renamed:- Sellafield.

UFO researchers everywhere are urged to consider very seriously the full implications of the texts of all the Cosmic Transmissions published by the Aetherius Society. That this information was first published in *Cosmic Voice* in 1957, just after the human blunder, should come to the attention of the scientific community, members of Parliament and the 'flying saucer' research fraternity.

Although the *New Scientist* admitted that it had been **"Scooped By A UFO"** with regards to the 1957/1958 Soviet nuclear disaster, this earlier 1957 Transmission about the UK accident at Windscale is not so well known.

The Aetherius Society should receive full credit for the proven publication of their Cosmic Transmissions, as well as many more regarding the dangers of radioactivity, nuclear experimentation and the overriding issue of nuclear waste disposal. Readers interested in pursuing these matters are recommended two books published by the Aetherius Society:-

(1) "YOU ARE RESPONSIBLE" (1961)
(2) "THE ATOMIC MISSION" (1973)

All books and lectures given by Dr. George King are available from the Aetherius Society, 757 Fulham Road, London, SW6 5UU.

[Press Release from the Aetherius Society - 1st March 1986]

March 1st, 1986....

FLYING SAUCER MESSAGES ON NUCLEAR DANGERS VALIDATED

The tides of controversy run high as fears and forthright opinions regarding the dangers of dumping nuclear waste are expressed publicly by politicians, scientists, environmentalists and the general public alike. The Aetherius Society, however, published Extra-Terrestrial warnings regarding nuclear power as early as 1955!

MESSAGE RE: SELLAFIELD COVER-UP .... ACCURATE

Information about the nuclear accident which took place at Windscale - now Sellafield - on October 10th, 1957, was published by The Aetherius Society in the journal "Cosmic Voice", Issue no. 13, December-January, 1957-58, in an article entitled "The Windscale Blunder". This information was received from an Extra-Terrestrial Source by Sir George King, Founder/President of The Aetherius Society on October 29th, 1957. This Source revealed that our scientists had not attempted to give us a true picture of the full damage done in this accident by the escape of plutonium dust, radio-active iodine and strontium 90.

The first official statement made by the then Prime Minister, now the Earl of Stockton, to the House of Commons on November 8th of that year, was as follows:

"There is no evidence that this accident has done any significant harm to any person, animal or property."

This statement was based upon the findings of two independent Committees of Inquiry consisting of scientists and experts set up by the Atomic Energy Authority on 15th October, 1957 and the Medical Research Council on October 29th, 1957 respectively.

Since then -

* British Nuclear Fuels Ltd. (B.N.F.L.) has paid out nearly £500,000 in compensation to the families of cancer victims among the workers at Sellafield.
* The incidence of leukaemia in people aged 25 and under, living in the community of Seascale near Sellafield, is ten times higher than the national average.

Such statistics show that the Prime Minister's statement is the result of a cover-up somewhere down the line by the scientists concerned - exactly as stated by an Extra-Terrestrial Source ten days earlier.

MESSAGE RE: RUSSIAN ATOMIC ACCIDENT .... ACCURATE

Another outstanding example of the validity of the Flying Saucer Message came in 1978 when the "New Scientist" had to admit that they had been "scooped by a U.F.O." regarding the now-famous 1958 atomic accident in the Soviet Union. This was hushed up successfully for 18 years from the world media – except that is for The Aetherius Society, which published the details of this event in "Cosmic Voice" Issue no. 16, June/July, 1958, after receiving details from an Extra-Terrestrial Source.

The Aetherius Society has a wealth of invaluable information on this and other major issues facing the world today, based on over six hundred Messages received by its Founder/President over 32 years, on a wide variety of subjects. It is now launching a nationwide series of lectures which answer the controversial "UFO Question" in full.

THE U.F.O. QUESTION ANSWERED

In the historic 1979 House of Lords Debate, the Earl of Cork and Orrery made the following famous quotation:

"I do not know what it implies to say that you do not believe in an unidentified flying object. You do not believe in the object? You do not believe in its flying? You do not believe it is unidentified? ....
The question is, what are they?"

- Why was there a spate of Flying Saucer sightings after the 2nd World War and up to the present day?
- Why have C.I.A. papers released under the Freedom of Information Act in 1979, which prove the existence of Flying Saucers, been officially ignored?
- Why has the Ministry of Defence not released its extensive U.F.O. files?
- Why and how is information given by Space Intelligences to Sir George King?
- What is the purpose of visits by Flying Saucers which have been reported throughout history, and when will they land openly among us?

The Aetherius Society will answer these and other questions in eight public meetings entitled "Flying Saucers – Their Message to Earth", to be held up and down the country from March 14th to May 7th, 1986. It will explain why these Spacecraft from other worlds should be more correctly termed I.F.O's (Identified Flying Objects). And it will inform the public that, regardless of belief or disbelief by people of this Earth, Flying Saucers are here to stay!

These meetings will be held at the venues listed opposite and further information may be obtained during the evenings from the local representatives listed, or from the European Headquarters Secretary, Dr. Richard Lawrence, or Public Relations Officer,

From the Press Release issued by the Aetherius Society in 1986.

AFTER CHERNOBYL

After the accident at Cheronbyl was detected in 1986 and declared to be the worst nuclear disaster the world had seen, there was great concern yet again about the safety of nuclear plants and the unpalatable issues concerning disposal of nuclear waste. The Observer, a newspaper in London, commissioned several writers to quickly publish a book about Chernobyl in 1986. The authors had this to say about the Ural mountain explosion of 1958:

"In December 1957, or perhaps the first week of January 1958 - the exact date is not known - what was widely accepted in the west as the worst nuclear accident prior to Chernobyl occurred on the edge of the Siberian plain at the plutonium-producing complex at Kyshtym. The US Defense Intelligence Agency (DIA) has identified Kyshtym as a reactor location that does not appear on the Soviet Union's published lists."
[From: THE WORST ACCIDENT IN THE WORLD - CHERNOBYL - THE END OF THE NUCLEAR DREAM]

(At that time, in 1986, the Soviet Union had not yet stated the proper date of the Kyshtym apocalypse. The admission was made on 16th June 1989) The book continued:

"In fact the Russians have never admitted that the accident occurred but from scientific journals, intelligence reports and refugee accounts it has been possible to put together a reasonable picture of what happened. It is certain that lethal radioactivity spread over hundreds of miles and thousands had to be evacuated and resettled.
  As in Chernobyl - but for different reasons, the first reports of the Kyshtym accident came from Scandinavia. Journalists in Denmark in April 1958, quoting diplomatic sources, wrote stories about a catastrophic accident inside the Soviet Union involving radioactive fallout."

Note that this book did not reference any of the Danish journalists, nor the journal of the Aetherius Society *Cosmic Voice*. As we have seen, the Cosmic Transmission that George King stated that he received was tape recorded in April 1958. The book continued:

"The stories ran in the *New York Times*, but the US Atomic Energy Commission said it had "no intelligence" of any such event. The next month, May, a newsletter published by the Munich-based Institute for the Study of the USSR, an arm of the propoganda unit of Radio Free Europe, commented on the 'unusual amount of attention' being given to radiation sickness in Soviet medical journals and even popular magazines. It said that on 9 January 1958, Radio Moscow had devoted a large segment to radiation sickness, describing in detail a list of possible preventive measures. This suggests that the accident happened around the end of December 1957.

"The accident was forgotten - **or deliberately suppressed in the west** - for nearly twenty years - until November 1976, when a Russian refugee biochemist, Zhores Medevedev, casually referred to the accident in the *New Scientist*. To his surprise he found that it was largely unknown. He suggested that the cause was probably an explosion, more likely chemical than nuclear, in radioactive wastes. His suggestion produced an hysterical reaction from western nuclear advocates because, at the time, the disposal of reactor wastes had become a major controversy in the western debate over nuclear power. It was an especially controversial issue in Britain. Medvedev was accused by intemperate British officials in the UK Atomic Energy Authority of being politically motivated in his explanation - especially as he had brought it up so long after the world had forgotten about it."

The truth of the matter was that the world did not even know about it, apart from the publication in *Cosmic Voice*. The West, including the CIA, had suppressed details. When the Soviet Union did admit an accident had happened, they stated that it had occurred in Kasli in 1957 in October, during which time they stated, there *had been no fatalities*. Either they got their facts wrong, or the October 1957 accident did not kill anyone immediately. But there had been large scale radioactive fallout which had contaminated land and lakes. Perhaps a later accident, which killed many people, may have resulted from an explosion of the accumulated waste, of a chemical nature, nevertheless attributable to nuclear products.

In his later book, "The Legacy of Chernobyl", Zhores Medvedev, in 1990, wrote:
""Even the most serious nuclear accident in the world before Chernobyl, the Kyshtym disaster in the Urals, which is now well documented in the Western literature, has not been mentioned *until recently in the Soviet Press."* [My italics]

"The Kyshtym disaster was a nuclear waste disposal accident at a military nuclear facility. Since it does not concern reactor technology which is the subject of this book, it will be considered only briefly here.

"Reprocessing spent nuclear fuel is part of the plutonium-producing industry and a special field of technology. The Kyshtym accident (also known as 'Nuclear disaster in the Urals) was the result of unsafe storage of reprocessed nuclear waste from military reactors and reprocessing plants which were in operation from 1948 in the area between the two old Ural towns of Kyshtym and Kasli, in the Chelyabinsk region............

"It is not known exactly how nuclear waste is disposed of in the Soviet Union. However, during the autumn of 1957 there was a thermal or chemical explosion in the waste disposal site and huge amounts of long-lived radionuclides, mainly strontium-90 and caesium-137 were blown over a large area in a north-easterly and westerly direction. An area as large as 1,000 - 2,000 square kilometers was heavily contaminated and evacuated. The level of contamination in the evacuated area reached between 2,000 and 4,000 curies per square kilometer."

===

Letters to Zhores Medvedev

In an effort to get clarification about the date of the accident (or accidents) I wrote to Dr. Zhores Medvedev on the 4th March 1990:

Dear Dr. Medvedev,
The nuclear accident that was admitted by the Soviet Union in June 1989 was supposed to have related to an explosion at Kasli in September 1957 during which, according to press reports, there were "no casualties". (References: Los Angeles Times 17 June 1989 / SCIENCE 23 June 1989)

I had been under the impression, from your book "NUCLEAR DISASTER IN THE URALS" that a worse tragedy had occurred at Kyshtym, probably in March 1958, that resulted in fatalities.
I have been wondering whether by admitting an earlier accident, the minister for 'Medium Machine Building', has deflected world attention away from the more serious accident that occurred later?

I would be very grateful for your comments on this supposition and for any further information you might have - to clarify this issue?

Medvedev, kindly replied to me on 2nd May 1990:

Dear Mr. Sirisena,
Thank you very much for your letter. My book describes the same accident - it was not known accurately when it happened. The Oak Ridge had classified it as 1957/58. Now it was reported that it did happen on 29 September 1957.
I have recently been in the USSR at a special Seminar of the Nuclear Society of the USSR, which discussed the accident. However, like with Chernobyl, the Soviet officials tried to minimise the medical aspects.

The force of the explosion was 100 tonnes of TNT and close parts of the area (near the disposal sites) had 300 - 500 R/h radioactivity.
It is impossible to believe that there were no health problems. But I suspect that mostly army and prisoners were used to clear the site and their health was not taken into account. I will write more serious analysis of new information later this year.
Please excuse for so messy reply - I was too busy in April, I was away most of March.
Yours sincerely,
Zhores Medvedev.

* * * *

The clarity that I sought about the dates was not evident in his reply. Therefore I wrote to Medvedev again on the 26th May 1990 for further elucidation about pinpointing the date, or dates, of several accidents..

Dear Dr. Medvedev,
I am grateful to you for having replied my letter (of 4 March 1990) on 2nd May 1990. It does raise some other questions which I hope you will be able to answer:

(1) Are you absolutely convinced that there was not another serious accident many months after September 1957?

(2) Your address to a Committee of the Supreme Soviet was reported in the *New Scientist* on 5 August 1989: it says, "Medvedev told the committee he first learnt of the accident from a brief Austrian press report in 1959......"!!!

Surely, this cannot be factual reporting? You have stated, both in your book and your second *New Scientist* article that you knew about the accident in 1958 when your professor offered you a job at a research station in the contaminated area. At least the report in *NATURE* (Vol 340, 3rd August 1989) seems to contain more accurate journalism.

(3) Can you recall exactly when in 1958 you first heard about an accident? Surely, one of the first questions you would have asked is: "When and where exactly did this terrible accident occur?" despite the fact that you state in your book (p 20): "At the time I was not interested in the exact date....." It seems very uncharacteristic of your goodself not to have been curious about the precise date of the explosion or explosions.

(4) The July 1989 IAEA press release on the USSR report by Nikipelov and 5 others gives facts and figures which are at great variance with your

research. I look forward to your more serious analysis later this year. Please let me know when and where it is published.

(5) Finally, the AAAS "SCIENCE" report of 16 April 1982, "Soviet Radwaste Spill Confirmed" stated that: "Medvedev speculated that the region was contaminated as a result of a nuclear explosion, caused by plutonium in waste material which reached critical mass."

Although you did consider many probable causes during your attempted reconstruction in your book, you did say, "It is useless to make any absolute assertions about the mechanism that set off the explosion in late 1957 or *early 1958*."
I well remember that one of John Hill's criticism in 1977 was that a chemical explosion could not possibly have occurred!
I feel that you have been vindicated despite all the subtle attempts to try and discredit your research between 1976 and 1989 on this matter.

I am still doubtful about many of the facts officially released by the USSR. I hope you can clarify the many points I have raised, especially the possibility of a second, serious accident between January and March 1958, as well as the fatal and medical consequences of the accident(s).

*   *   *   *   *   *   *   *   *   *

A reply from Zhores Medvedev, dated 19 June 1990, was received by me in due course.

Dear Ananda L. Sirisena,
Thank you for your letter of May 26, 1990.
New Scientist did use for an article information from BBC Monitoring Service (translation of Soviet radio broadcasts) and this source made them to make many mistakes. I found Austrian newspaper only in 1980 when my book was already published. New Scientist did not try to verify the story - it was their fault.
Apparently Kyshtym could be a source of several different accidents. However one which did happen in September, 1957 was the most serious I knew about since 1958 when Prof. V.M. Kletchkovsky started to make some steps to set up an experimental station there - I told about this in my book.
My more detailed report on Kyshtym is written in Russian and now sent to two Soviet magazines, Ural and Energija,
With all best wishes.
Yours sincerely.

Zhores A. Medvedev

I did not write to Medvedev again as I had not been able to ascertain the date of an accident in the first quarter of 1958 directly from him. He admitted that "Kyshtym could be a source of several different accidents" but did not seem to be certain or clear about the timeframe of January to March 1958. Although he had stated in his first *New Scientist* article that an accident had happened in 1958, he did not give a precise date. He had written: "A tragic catastrophe occurred in 1958......"

(Medvedev passed away in November 2018 in London. Obituaries appeared in the Times, Telegraph and the Guardian, as well as the New York Times.)

===

An acquaintance of mine, David Capraro, from the Michigan Branch of the Aetherius Society in USA, sent me something truly interesting and quite revealing. An extract from :

HEARINGS BEFORE A SUBCOMMITTEE OF THE COMMITTEE ON FOREIGN RELATIONS - UNITED STATES SENATE CONTROL AND REDUCTION OF ARMAMENTS - 1959

The Hearings considered the detection of an explosion in the Ural Mountains on *25th March 1958*. Here is an extract of the relevant section:

*   *   *   *

Senator HUMPHREY. How did they detect this explosion 5,000 miles away in the Ural Mountains on March 25 in the Soviet Union?

Dr. HAN BETHE. By seismographs

Senator HUMPHREY. They did not know that the Soviets were going to explode it?

Senator HICKENLOOPER. I was going to get into that a little later when we get to the seismograph people. I do not know, but I have an impression that they could not identify it necessarily as an underground explosion. They suspected that it might have been an underground explosion because an earthquake had not occurred in that area for 40 years, and that raised a question: Is that an explosion or is it an earthquake after 40 years?

Dr. BETHE. That is precisely right.

Senator HICKENLOOPER. Yes. Then when Russia verified that they had exploded it, they said, "We caught the wiggle on the seismograph."

Dr. BETHE. They caught that wiggle unannounced.

Senator HICKENLOOPER. That is right.

Dr. BETHE. And the explosion was a few kilotons and the wiggle was caught unannounced, and since it was in an aseismic region --.....

* *

We can see from this extract in Hearings in the Senate, discussions between Senators Hubert H. Humphrey (of Minnesota) and Bourke B. Hickenlooper (of Iowa) and their questions to Dr. Han Bethe, professor of physics at Cornell University that they are struggling to understand a seismograph "wiggle" that had been detected on 25th March 1958 in the Ural Mountains!

Their discussion centred around differentiating an 'underground explosion' with a naturally occurring earthquake. When the USSR announced that an accident had taken place in October 1957, they did not state anything about an explosion on 25th March 1958.

So it seems that there were 2 major events in the Ural Mountains:

29 September 1957

and

25 March 1958

Both accidents seem to have happened in the Ural Mountains area, between Kasli and Kyshtym.

Dr. George King's announcement in April 1958 was proven to be uncannily accurate.

NEW SCIENTIST SAYS IT HAD BEEN "SCOOPED BY A UFO"!

PRESS CUTTING
NEW SCIENTIST - Feedback p. 241
DATE
27th April 1978

Scooped by a UFO

In among the claims that "Flying Saucers are real, and physical, are friendly, are extraterrestrial" and exhortations that we should "demand the truth", the June/July 1958 issue of *Cosmic Voice* contained a curious tale of UFO communication.

Medium George King reported that on 18 April of that year he had received a transmission from flying saucers in "Mars Sector 6" reporting that "Owing to the atomic accident just recently in the USSR, a great amount of radioactivity . . . has been released into the atmosphere". And we thought *New Scientist* was the first to report it—in 1976 (vol 72, p 264)!

The New Scientist ultimately confessed that it had been **'scooped by a UFO'**. It admitted this fact in April 1978 twenty years after the event initially reported by *Cosmic Voice*.

PART THREE

The Moon and beyond...... unusual findings

One of the first books I borrowed on the subject of unidentified flying objects, after my sighting of 8th July 1964, from the local library was entitled:

"The Sky People" written by Brinsley Le Poer Trench and first published in 1960, four years before I became interested in the subject.

At the time I did not know that the author was none other than the Earl of Clancarty, who sat in the House of Lords. Lord Clancarty was instrumental in organising and participating in the House of Lords UFO Debate on 18 January 1979.

The back cover of "The House of Lords UFO Debate" had a pertinent question from him:

"Is it not time that Her Majesty's Government informed our people of what they know about UFOs? I think it is time our people were told the truth."
             - LORD CLANCARTY

MASSIVE VIMANA OVER THE AWE

> # The House of Lords UFO Debate.
> ## Illustrated, Full Transcript with Preface by Lord Clancarty (Brinsley le Poer Trench) and Notes by John Michell.

The inside cover stated:
Crown Copyright text of the debate reproduced by permission of *Hansard*

UFO photograph kindly supplied by the Aetherius Society where Founder Dr. George King, claims many UFO contacts, one of which provided the specifications for this model

This edition first published in 1979, showing the back cover.

> "Is it not time that Her Majesty's Goverment informed our people of what they know about UFOs? I think it is time our people were told the truth."
> -Lord CLANCARTY.

The recent debate on unidentified flying objects (UFOs) in the House of Lords was the first to be held on this subject by any national legislative body. The motion, calling upon the Government to promote international study of the rapidly growing UFO problem, was introduced to the Upper Chamber of the British Parliament by the Earl of Clancarty, better known as the pioneer UFO writer, Brinsley le Poer Trench.

Together with other speakers in the debate, notably the Earl of Kimberley, former Liberal spokesman on aerospace, Clancarty urges the Government to publish their secret files of UFO records and to reveal what is officially known about the phenomenon. His restrained, scholarly opening speech brings a variety of interesting responses from fellow peers. Contributions include charges of official UFO-news suppression, noble theories of UFO origins, accounts of members' sightings and a theological intervention by the Bishop of Norwich. Marginal notes in this edition provide background information on the UFO cases and other matters referred to in this debate, and there are many relevant illustrations.

Open Head Press/Pentacle Books
ISBN 0 9506772 0 5
Price £2.95

Other books I found in various libraries were written by American major Donald E. Keyhoe. Quickly, I had read the following books by Keyhoe:
The Flying Saucers Are Real
Flying Saucers - Top Secret
Flying Saucers From Outer Space

FLYING SAUCERS AND THE US AIR FORCE
I became aware of the controversy about ufos throughout the world, from the US Air Force Project Blue Book (preceded by Project Saucer, Project Sign and Project Grudge) through to its disbanding in 1968/69, after the University of Colorado study known as the Condon Report.

It was in 1960 that the US Air Force officially sanctioned a book written by spokesman Lawrence J. Tacker called: **"Flying Saucers And The US Air Force - The Official Air Force Story"**

In one section of Tacker's book was the following letter published, attached to two Transmissions delivered through George King:

"Dear Sir,
I accuse the press of this world of suppressing the truth concerning the danger of atomic explosions. Why have they not published the truth concerning the danger of radiation, causing chain reaction. In many cases, air crashes are due to this radiation, mysterious explosions in ships, fires breaking out, on land and sea, which cannot be accounted for by ordinary means.
"Doctors and scientists try to explain it away by calling it a phobia, to ease their conscience. Bluffing the masses, fooling the people, denying them the truth, which has been given to them. Hypnotizing the people, pandering to man's ignorance of the true position.
"The press and editors have had the truth put before them, why have they not published these warnings? Those responsible for this, will have to account for this suppression when passing into the next sphere of existence. You had the power of the Press to tell the truth, you have failed in your duty of publishing these great truths."

Lt. Colonel Lawrence Tacker had written, "This is a lengthy letter with a quoted message from Venus warning the people on Earth of their responsibilities in space." Lawrence J. Tacker republished other extracts from a Transmission - stated by George King to have been delivered by a communicator given the codename "Mars Sector 6" and tape recorded at the time, on 16th August 1958:

MARS SECTOR 6

"This is Mars Sector 6 reporting from Satellite No. 3 now in Observation Orbit— "Subject: **TREAD CAREFULLY YE MEN!**
"Terra today stands on the very brink of the first attempt to probe the mysteries of outer space.
"The men of science just took it for granted that the people who inhabit other Planets and *have used your Moon as a base for nineteen million years*, would welcome them with open arms.
"Either that—or they cared not whether the users of the Moon wish their trespass!
"Although the bases of the Moon have been used primarily so that Terra should be protected from her own wrong-doing, *those who asked us not knew of our positions upon Luna.* Those who did not know of our positions were ignorant *only because they chose to hide their greying heads beneath the sands of their own dogmatic ignorance.*

"According to our agents, the United States of America intend—quite shortly—to launch a rocket towards Luna. This is to be followed soon afterwards by an attempt which will be made by Russia. In neither case has our sanction been sought.
"But I would remind you, Sirs, that when you place a vehicle in that position in space you call—free-fall, **responsibility towards all life and towards the Cosmic Whole is increased three million times.**
"To ignore this warning will not alter the fact! You have been told!
"If you try, at any time, to bombard the Moon with an explosive weapon you must reap the inevitable—listen to that, Terra! —**inevitable consequences.**
"If you, or any other country upon Terra make any attempt to bombard the Moon or any other inhabited Planet or Satellite, with explosive weapons, you will reap the consequences almost at once!
"You may turn what deaf ear you wish to this. **The fact is, and forever will remain so.**
"I would say to American scientists, immediately you venture outside the gravitational field of your own Planet, Terra, your behaviour will be most carefully watched. Not by people from Mars or Venus but by greater people than these—**by the Supreme Lords of Karma.** By the self-same Mighty Galactic Beings who guarantee that the Law of Action and Reaction is perfect!
"If you go into Space you must behave yourselves. If you do not do so, **Divine Justice is liable to strike like lightning.**

"Those of you who can think for yourselves, must see the logic in this. Must be eternally grateful for this kindly advice. Because, Men of Science, this **is** advice—and not warning.

"If you murder another Earth man, your Karma will demand its balance—but it may do this some time after. If you murder any other Intelligence from a more highly advanced Planet than your own—your Karma must find its balance. **It will do this at once.**

"I would advise you before you attempt to throw an atomic missile at your Moon, to think well upon the teachings of the Master you **say** you follow. He stated that, 'He who lives by the sword, shall die by the sword.'

"Throw a bomb into the serene face of Luna, Terra, and you will die! In the self-same way Karma will extract balance. **This is the Law, whether you like it or not! Whether you believe it or not!**

"In this respect now, ignorance can no longer be your glib excuse.

"FOR—I HAVE SPOKEN!

"This Transmission was an emergency Transmission to the Space scientists of Terra.

"My friends—if you ever do circumnavigate Luna please realise that it is the people on the other Planets who have **allowed** you to do this. In return, you must behave yourselves—in a very definite, very controlled way, or else you must be prepared to take the Divine consequences.

"Pain is the greatest teacher but it is not the only teacher.

"May God bless the peacemakers upon Terra.

"This Transmission came from Mars Sector 6, from Satellite No. 3, now in Observation Orbit—Luna. With the Sanction and Authority of Interplanetary Parliament based upon the Planet Saturn.

"WITH THE SANCTION AND AUTHORITY OF THE SUPREME LORDS OF KARMA.

"Through Primary Terrestrial Mental Channel.

"All Transmissions now discontinued."

THE MASTER AETHERIUS SPEAKS TO EARTH

THE MASTER AETHERIUS
"Yes! It is so! You can see that but a few people have been able, by their unselfish efforts, to do a great amount of good for Terra as a whole.
"Please go on, dear friends—to your own Salvation.
"I tell you this, in these days, **Salvation is a reward for service.** Gone are the days when a man upon Terra is considered right when he divorces himself from humanity as a whole and spends his life in private devotion and meditation.
"I am not saying, of course, that private devotion or meditation is in any way wrong— but service among people is the order of this present time. Note that—dear friends—**service among people.** Such is the precarious state of Terra as a whole, that service is needed **within** the mass of humanity.
"It is for this reason that our major approaches have been made to those who may appear to all intents and purposes to be ordinary individuals.
"We have been asked several times why we do not channel our approach through scientific organisations. My answer to that must be that the majority—not all—but the majority of Terrestrial scientists have minds likened to a cup filled with liquid which cannot hold anything more. Any other knowledge offered to the minds of certain scientists upon Terra would be purely and completely representative of a waste of mental energy.
"When the cup is full, more liquid is a superfluity for it runneth over.
"It is for this reason that we are making an approach to the masses, in dozens of different ways—some apparent, some not so apparent. It is because the ordinary decent, right-thinking, World Citizens—note that please—WORLD CITIZENS—are the people who will have to act as one great whole, in order to put right this terrible chaos which now reigns upon your Earth.
"These are the people who suffer by this chaos. In some countries they suffer starvation and disease. In other countries they suffer an ignorance which has been specially planned—the foulest move of all, this! They suffer dictatorship in other countries. They are conditioned and have been, throughout the centuries. It is the ordinary man who is the sufferer when war comes. The ordinary man does not gain anything, one way or the other. He is the loser in war—and also the person conditioned in Peace.
"It is for this reason that we are making our main approach to the ordinary individual because the Lords of Karma have stated beyond all doubt, that it is this sufferer who will eventually break the bond which has bound him as a slave to dreadful orthodox conditioning for many lives.

"The revolution will be a mental one. It will be a Renaissance. It will be a **transmutation of basic thought into Spiritual action.** Note that—A TRANSMUTATION OF BASIC THOUGHT INTO SPIRITUAL ACTION. That is what it will be! That is why our approach has been directed to you, who are the backbone of your Earth. To you, who are on the mental Realms and to you who are the backbone of your Spiritual Realms.

"We make our main approach to you and in doing so remind you again, of your great responsibility to your Earth and to those who are deaf and blind—in the higher sense—upon your Earth.

"These need your prayers and your healing, for they are the great black ones. Their magic has been specially designed throughout the centuries to make powerful castles for themselves. They have done this. Now they manipulate Governments, whole countries and these countries obey like so many puppets at the bottom of the strings in a marionette show!

"This dark group will be taken from the centre of your Earth but dear friends, please, PLEASE, do not let their evil schemes bear fruit **before** they are taken from it. By that I mean, that the great conspirators are in your midst. They have been there for centuries. You have danced to their tune! The whole propaganda organisation throughout all Earth, which produces either an uneasy Peace or a war or a cold war or fear or famine, is the tool used by these dark few among you. They are very powerful for they manipulate the monetary wealth of Terra. This gives them almost unlimited power upon the surface of Terra.

"But note this, Terra! The time of their trial is nigh! **The time when a great beam of understanding and transmuting light,** which will be thrown deep into the heart of this foul, black, cancerous growth within your Earth, **is shortly due to come.**

"The dawn, my friends, will soon break. "Be ready for it—when it does so!

"This is another main reason why we have directed our major appeal through Primary Terrestrial Mental Channel and **why this major appeal has over-ruled all other contacts, all other appeals. Why we have directed it towards the decent World Citizen, in the hope that he will allow his decency to rise uppermost within his heart and will sink petty difference, burn up so-called individuality in the fire of total co-operation and be prepared for the coming of the great transmuting light.**

"I said a few moments ago, that you must not allow the plans of the few dark ones to bear fruit. By this I mean that, even at this very moment they are trying to stir up strife within this Earth of yours. To cause a war between countries and hate to exist between white men, yellow men and coloured men. They are trying to do this!

"They will succeed. They will succeed in bringing about a wholesale war to the face of your Globe. They will succeed in bringing about an atomic war to the face of your Globe, which will destroy and horribly mutate your children for a hundred generations—UNLESS— **you stop them!** Unless you stop them by non-co-operation with their foul plans.

"This group—they are known to some as the Silence Group—have been responsible for the present conditions upon Terra to some extent but you, the ordinary men have been responsible to an even greater extent, for allowing this to happen by your own apathy. **By your own apathy!**

"Stop it, dear friends—NOW—by becoming free in your thinking. By choosing a Master you really believe in, whether it be Jesus, Buddha or Krishna or whoever it may be AND BY LIVING THOSE TEACHINGS.

"In this way—**in this only way**—will you, the decent World Citizen, be instrumental in saving yourselves great pain and suffering.

"We do not want to see a war upon Terra and if it did come to this, we could only intervene directly with our energies through Terrestrial people **or those people who appear to be Terrestrial people.**

"If these people do not tune into our Energies and allow themselves to be used freely as channels, then by the Karmic Law, by the Great Cosmic Law, we cannot intervene. Because, you see, Terra, you have put yourself in great Spiritual debt.

"Each and every man has only a certain amount of energy available to him through each and every incarnation. Each and every Planet has only a certain very definite and measured amount of energy available for its use. Terra has already overstepped this mark.

"You are now in great debt, so therefore this makes intervention extremely difficult.

Know this! Take it deep into your hearts—NOW—TONIGHT. Take it home with you. And you on the higher Planes who are here, take it deep into your Souls—NOW!

"Realise it beyond all doubt. Know that there are not two ways open to you. There is but one way—that is to get back to the Laws given to you by numerous different teachers throughout the ages. Teachers who have sacrificed Heavenly bliss—as you would call it—on your behalf.

"In chaos do the dark ones live—not in Peace. In darkness do these evil plotters scheme—not in Light.

"Wake up, Terrestrial man, to the things which are happening beneath your very noses, at this moment. When you have woken up, do something about this in a peaceful manner. In a humble manner but in a definite manner. In a strong manner.

"This is why we come to you because you, the ordinary man, has, suffered at the hands of the few dark ones.

"**The time is ripe for you to break the bonds of this conditioning.
"Live the Laws of whatever Master you choose and bring Light and a great Golden Age to the surface of your Planet.**
"Either that—or reject this advice and go on in your own apathetic manner and you will have devastating bombs landing upon your cities throughout the World.
"You will have a flip in the axis of this World of yours, causing a movement of at least 75 per cent of all water masses on Earth. Causing annihilation in less than 15 minutes, of at least 90 per cent of all humanoid life.
"**Yes—you stand now upon the cross-roads of decision.**
"What will your decision be?
"Apathy—or TRANSMUTATION? "Pain and suffering—or PEACE? "Starvation—or PLENTY?
"This is what you have to decide upon—and act upon your decision.
"By your standards I would be considered to be a person of some experience. I have lived upon hundreds of different inhabited Worlds throughout the Solar and Galactic Systems. I have lived even among you people upon Terra, at different times.
"You would think that I am ancient. I am Ancient—by your standards. Yet never, dear friends, in the whole of this experience, have I seen people who have been given greater opportunity than that offered to you now.
"**Your opportunities are Divine—wholly Divine.**
"**You can advance a thousand lives in the next few years—or go back ten thousand.**
"**I leave you now with that choice—for it is yours to make—and only you can make it.**
"Make it well, Oh brothers. MAKE IT WELL!

===

One of the excerpts from these Transmissions stated:

"Although the bases of the Moon have been used primarily so that Terra should be protected from her own wrong-doing, those who asked us not, knew of our positions upon Luna. Those who did not know of our positions were ignorant only because they chose to hide their greying heads beneath the sands of their own dogmatic ignorance."

Moon pictures

The possibility of alien bases upon our moon has been raised again and again since our exploration of the moon started. A technical paper, in the

Journal of Space Exploration, published in 2017, showed photographs taken by the Lunar Reconnaissance Orbiter (LRO) in a crater of our lunar globe called Paracelsus C.

The objects had been originally photographed by the astronauts aboard Apollo 15 - David Scott, Alfred Worden and James Irwin in 1971.

[APOLLO 15 IMAGE AS15-P-8868-003 OF CRATER PARACELSUS-C]

Apollo 15 was the fourth mission to land men on the Moon. This mission was the first flight of the Lunar Roving Vehicle (LRV) which astronauts used to explore the geology of the Hadley Rille/Apennine region. The LRV allowed Apollo 15, 16 and 17 astronauts to venture further from the Lunar Module than in previous missions. Total surface traverses increased from hundreds of meters during earlier missions to tens of kilometers during Apollo 15 and 16 and just over 100 kilometers during Apollo 17. However, Apollo 15 did not explore any of the craters which make up the series known as Paracelsus.

The photo shown above - AS15-P-8868-003 - is only one of several pictures taken by the Apollo 15 astronauts over this region of the moon. Images AS15-P-8868-001 through to 008 all captured these strange, wall-like features; 8 images in total. The reader is shown here a series of enlargements of just one of these: AS15-P-8868-003. Successive enlargements of the Apollo 15 image show three peculiar objects lying on the moon's surface. It has been ascertained that they are not the remnants of any terrestrial rocket that crash landed in the area.

MASSIVE VIMANA OVER THE AWE

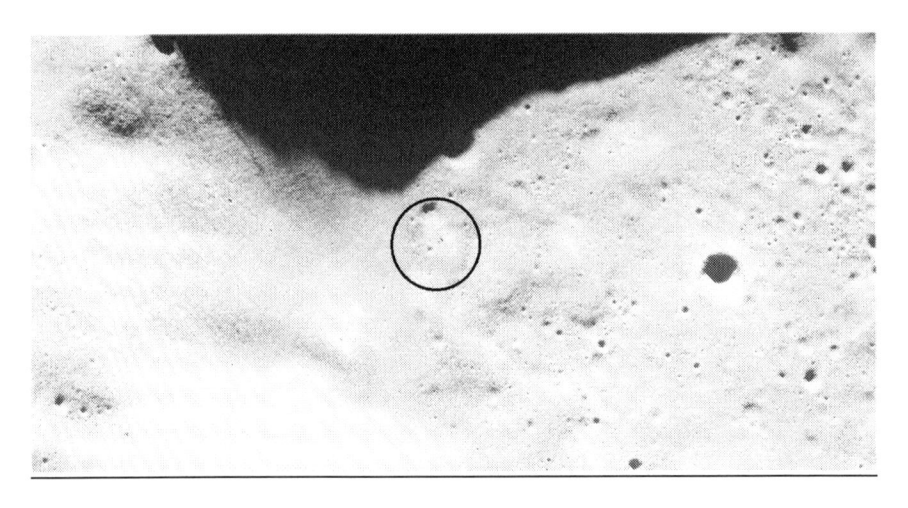

The circled are in the picture above shows the region in Paracelsus C which is of interest.

Clearly visible in this image are the unusual objects that look like "walls".

MASSIVE VIMANA OVER THE AWE

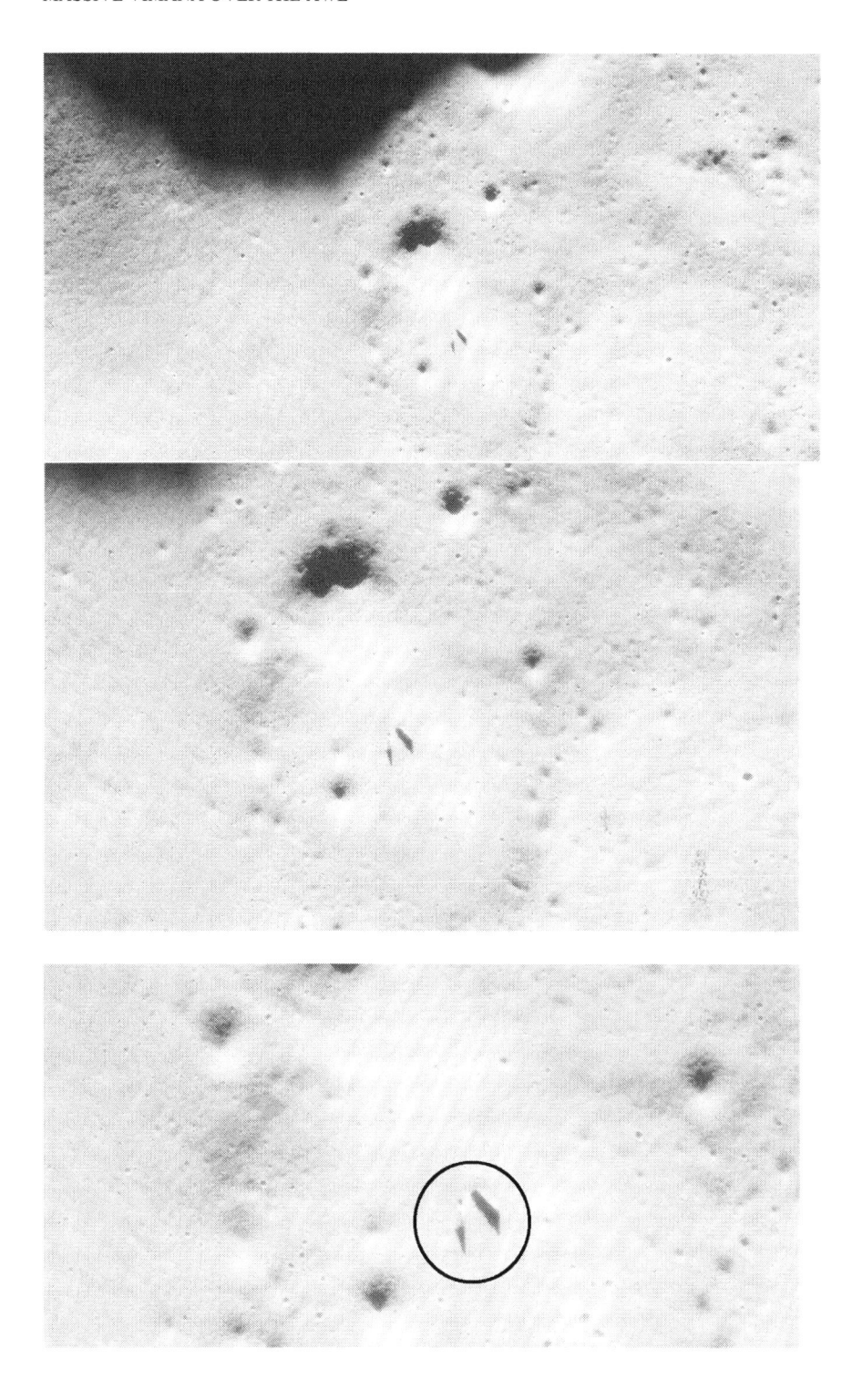

Above photos were taken by the crew of Apollo 15 in 1971. More recent, close-up, higher resolution images taken by the Lunar Reconnaissance Orbiter (LRO) shows the same objects in much greater detail. As surprising as it might seem, a technical paper published in *The Journal of Space Exploration* in 2017 indicates an unresolved mystery in the crater known as Paracelsus C. Readers who are interested in the analysis conducted by an image processing expert are encouraged to read the complete paper, obtainable from this link:

https://www.researchgate.net/publication/310506051_Image_Analysis_of_Unusual_Structures_on_the_Far_Side_of_the_Moon_in_the_Crater_Paracelsus_C

1 mpp 150 meters	
	LUNAR RECONNAISSANCE OBSERVER **FRAME M118769870L** **TAKEN ON 22nd JANUARY 2010**

[The objects photographed by the Apollo 15 astronauts were rephotographed by the Lunar Reconnaissance Orbiter (LRO) in much greater detail. Shown here is a portion of Image No. M118769870L, boxed in a square 150 meters in size, so as to provide a more precise indication of their actual size. The antiquity of these objects is demonstrated by the apparent meteor strikes on both large objects.]

The LRO has taken 5 different images of these strange, wall-like features on the moon. The paper quoted above reveals more mysterious facts about the crater and its contents. Could these have been part of an ancient alien base on our moon?

All images courtesy of NASA. The orientation of the LRO image above is similar to the Apollo 15 images.

The first page of the paper published in the Journal of Space Exploration is shown below. It makes for fascinating reading as the analysis uses the digital information from several of the LRO images to build a 3-dimensional over-arching view of that part of the crater Paracelsus-C.

[Image M118769870L - showing the region in context]

MASSIVE VIMANA OVER THE AWE

MASSIVE VIMANA OVER THE AWE

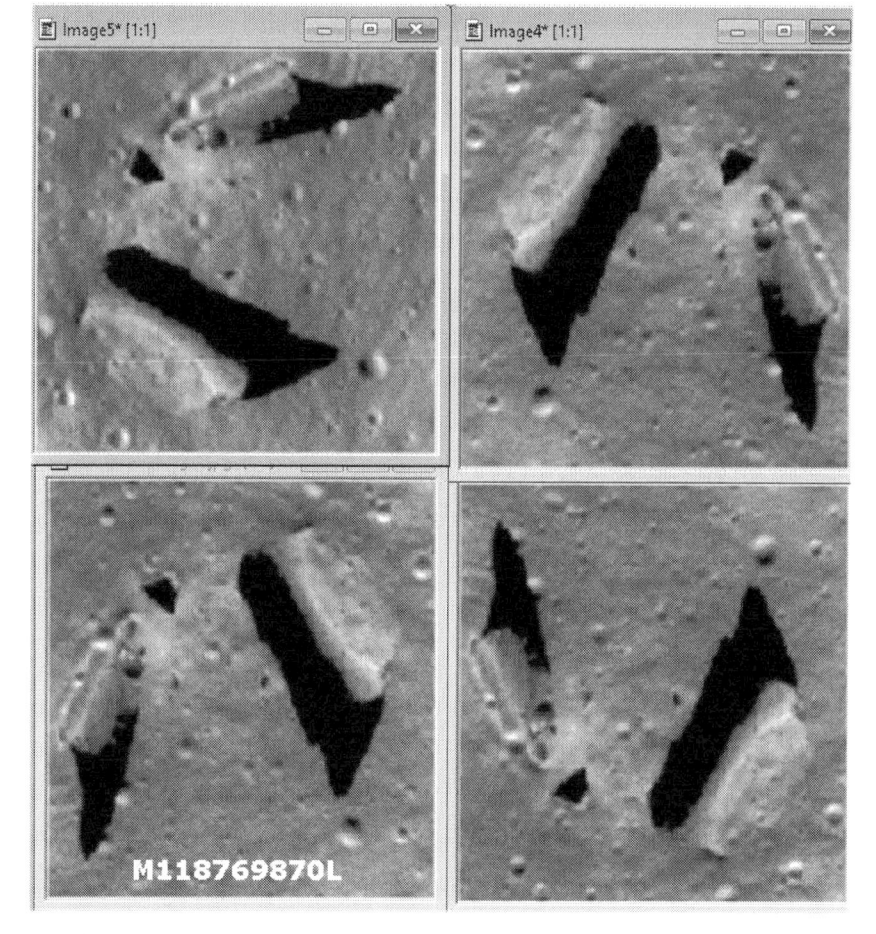

M118769870L

NASA has released 5 Lunar Reconnaissance Orbiter photos of these unusual objects, dated as follows:

M118769870L - 22nd January 2010

M1115441699L - 14th February 2013

M1153132512R - 26th April 2014

M1168450258l - 20th October 2014

M1237871462R - 1st January 2017

Journal of Space Exploration

Research | Vol 5 Iss 2

Image Analysis of Unusual Structures on the Far Side of the Moon in the Crater Paracelsus C

Mark J Carlotto[*], Francis L Ridge and Ananda L Sirisena

The Lunascan Project and Society for Planetary SETI Research, Tennessee, USA

[*]**Corresponding author:** Carlotto MJ, The Lunascan Project, Society for Planetary SETI Research, Tennessee, USA, Tel: 978-807-7758; E-mail: mark@carlotto.us

Abstract

The authors present an analysis of Apollo 15 and Lunar Reconnaissance Orbiter images of two unusual features in the crater Paracelsus C on the far side of the moon. At first glance these structures appear to be walls or towers on the lunar surface. By combining multiple images, we show the larger feature, oriented in a northeast/southwest direction, is not simply a wall but two walls on either side of a narrow valley or "passageway". Using single image shape from shading and 3D terrain visualization we show in a computer-generated perspective view looking northeast that the southwest end appears to be the entrance to the passageway. A reverse angle view looking southwest shows the passageway ending at a rise of terrain at the other end, possibly leading underground. The terrain surrounding the two structures is not flat but appears "excavated" by some unknown mechanism, natural or artificial. It is shown that these objects are visually different from the lunar background because their underlying structure is different.

Keywords: Paracelsus C; Moon; Lunar

Received: July 26, 2016; Accepted: September 20, 2016; Published: September 30, 2016

Introduction

The search for extra-terrestrial intelligence (SETI) began in the 1960s with radio-telescopes and has, to date, produced no positive evidence of its existence. During these early years of SETI, Sagan [1] spoke about the possibility of extraterrestrial visitation, "It is not out of the question that artifacts of these visits still exist, or even that some kind of base is maintained (possibly automatically) within the solar system to provide continuity for successive expeditions. Because of weathering and the possibility of detection and interference by the inhabitants of the Earth, it would be preferable not to erect such a base on the Earth's surface. The Moon seems one reasonable alternative. Forthcoming high resolution photographic reconnaissance of the Moon from space vehicles – particularly of the back side – might bear these possibilities in mind".

THE VIKING PROBES TO MARS

Science in general and biology in particular, is driven by the belief that life on Earth started through a series of *random* chemical combinations or *accidents of nature* that moulded together to form the living components. The belief is that from a single-celled organism, life evolved to patterns of multi-cellular intricate life-forms, culminating in a pinnacle as us humans - the homo sapiens species, over a very long period of time.

Peculiarly, this assumption is tacitly accepted without regard to alternatives, or without asking the simple question: "Where do humans evolve to next?" Either way, our theory on the evolution of life is accepted by science without regard to the fact that we have had only one data set to work with, namely life on Earth. What about life on other planets? Even the answer to this question is looked at in a strangely egocentric fashion.

The "life experiments" on Mars, conducted by the Viking landers in 1976 apparently gave unmistakable signals for living organisms in the soil of the red planet. The results have been brushed under a carpet of 'chemical' explanations.

One of the scientists who designed the "Labelled Release" experiment for the Viking landers has stated that it did find signs of microbial life in the soil of our neighbouring planet Mars. Dr. Gilbert Levin has never given up on that scientific conclusion. I remain puzzled as to why NASA took the position that the reactions observed by the portable laboratories of Viking 1 and Viking 2 were simply chemical reactions. The scientific evidence suggests otherwise.

PERPLEXING CONFIGURATION OF MOUNDS ON MARS

In the northern part of Mars known as Cydonia, there are several mounds which form a ground pattern that seems to be mathematically precise. On average, these mounds are around the size of the great pyramid at Giza in Egypt. They are of different size and shape and may have been eroded over a very long time, possibly millions of years. The photo below shows part of Frame 35A72, taken in 1976.

The mound configuration on Mars in the Cydonia region - 1976 Viking frame

Notice the small, bright features scattered in an apparently random fashion. The late Dr. Horace Crater performed an analysis of the positioning of these high albedo mounds and was surprised to see that they formed an intriguing layout. Dr. Crater had been a professor of physics for 40 years at the University of Tennessee Space Institute in USA, until his demise in 2017. He was able to ascertain that the angles between the mounds which he labelled A, B, D, E, F and G were suggestive of a mathematical set of repeating angles and triangles. He first published a paper about this configuration in 1999 in the Journal of Scientific Exploration, written together with professor Stanley McDaniel of Sonoma State University. At that time, only the pictures taken by NASA's 1976 Viking spacecraft to Mars were available for researchers and many members of the public were waiting for newer photos from a later set of rockets which were due to take off towards Mars.

NASA confirmed that the features in Cydonia truly existed when MGS - Mars Global Surveyor started its mapping mission in 1999. Unsurprisingly, the European Space Agency also rephotographed Cydonia and released pictures of the area in 2003, which confirm that the pattern formed by the mounds do exist. Later, in 2008, NASA's Mars Reconnaissance Orbiter (MRO) produced photos with the highest resolution, ten times better than the original, 1976 Viking photos.

Another surprise: line GA is parallel to line EB.
Line EG is parallel to line BA.
The parallelogram formed by GABE is striking.
Dr. Crater decided to analyse all the angles in this formation of five
mounds, which he called "The Pentad".

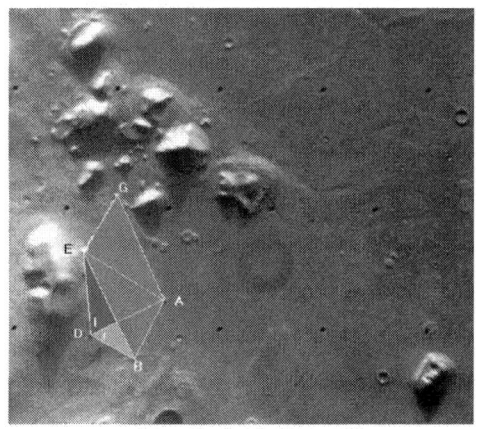

Prepared by Ananda Sirisena

Approximate sizes of the mounds, which are of different shape, are as follows:

Mound A = 280 metres by 380 metres
Mound B = 170 metres by 180 metres
Mound D = 290 metres by 420 metres
Mound E = 230 metres by 250 metres
Mound G = 240 metres by 480 metres

These sizes are estimated from an image taken by the MRO on 13th September 2014.
In comparison, the large pyramid at Giza in Egypt has a square base measured out to be 230 metres by 230 metres.
The mounds form a grid-like pattern. Is this a natural coincidence or is this indicative of extraterrestrial intervention on our neighbouring planet?

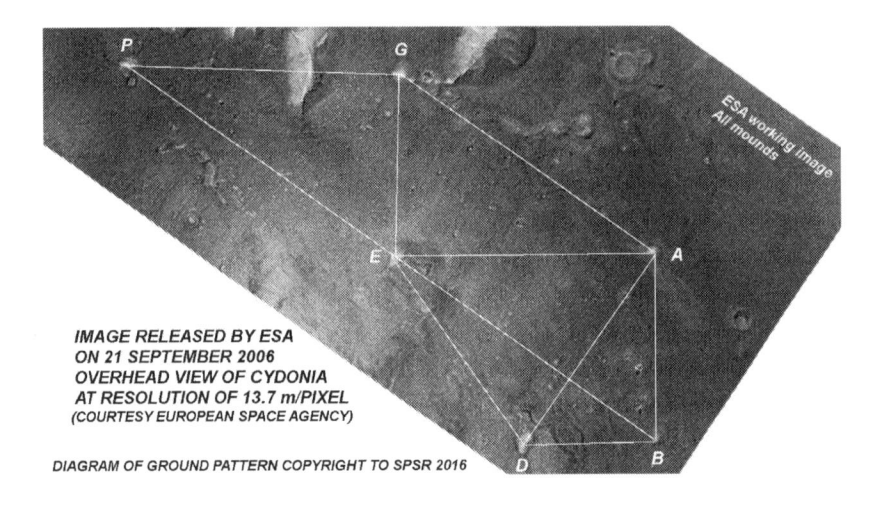

IMAGE RELEASED BY ESA ON 21 SEPTEMBER 2006 OVERHEAD VIEW OF CYDONIA AT RESOLUTION OF 13.7 m/PIXEL (COURTESY EUROPEAN SPACE AGENCY)

DIAGRAM OF GROUND PATTERN COPYRIGHT TO SPSR 2016

Professor Horace Crater has named the five-sided figure GEDBA the "Pentad" and the six-sided figure PGABDE the "Hexad". Precise measurements made by Crater and McDaniel and a superb mathematical analysis shows that these six mounds may have been laid out in an intelligent fashion. Does this prove that there was, or is, intelligence on Mars? We do not know the answer to the question with hundred percent certainty; further study of the region would be required to take this puzzle further. Many geologists believe that these features on Mars are very ancient - may be millions and millions of years old.

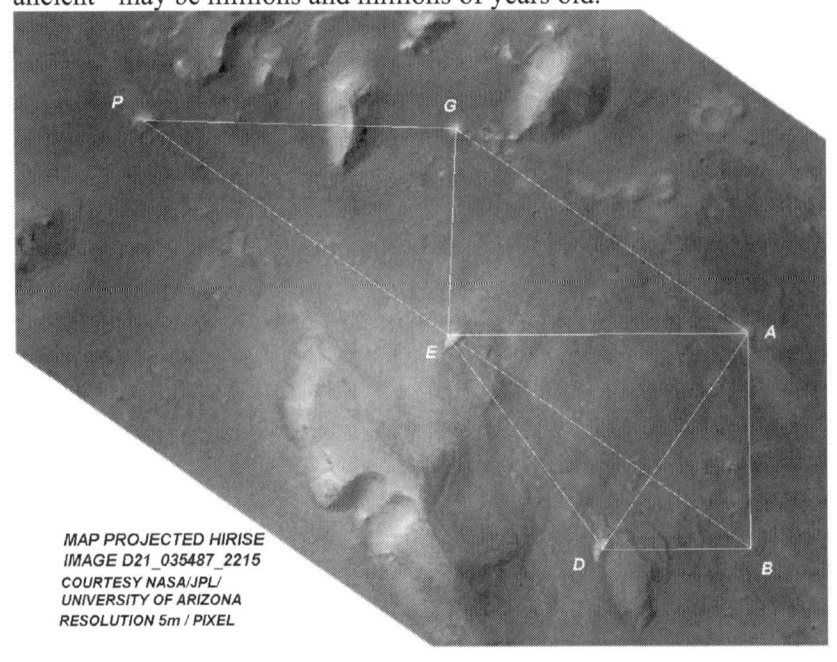

MAP PROJECTED HIRISE IMAGE D21_035487_2215 COURTESY NASA/JPL/ UNIVERSITY OF ARIZONA RESOLUTION 5m / PIXEL

MRO image released in 2014 - 5 metres per pixel

HIRISE IMAGE 2014

Prepared by Ananda Sirisena 2017

The above picture is the highest resolution image of the Cydonia region so far released by NASA. At 5 meters per pixel it clearly shows the six mounds that form the precise configuration.

Three sets of different images from different spacecraft now confirm the stunning discovery made by professors Horace Crater and Stanley McDaniel.

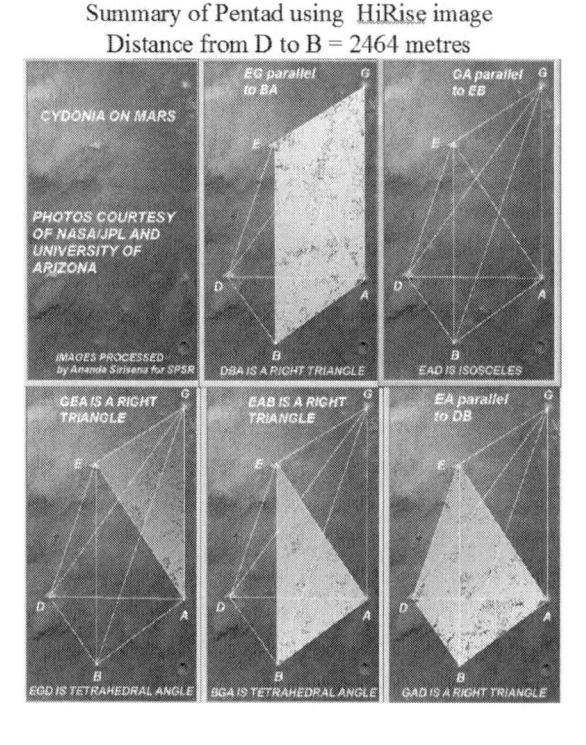

Summary of Pentad using HiRise image
Distance from D to B = 2464 metres

[Mathematical analysis completed by late professor of physics at the University of Tennessee Space Institute - Dr. Horace Crater.]

If anyone can explain how these six mounds on Mars, forming the hexad, came to be positioned, please contact the author at the email address below. Late professor of physics, Dr. Horace Crater performed the original analysis and no one has been able to solve the mystery since his initial paper. Professor Stanley McDaniel has stated his finding that the mounds sit on a "square-root-two grid.". McDaniel's observation needs an explanation from planetary scientists and martian areologists.

Notice the parallel lines and the right-angled triangles - perhaps a layout indicative of intelligence? I maintain that the complete analysis done by the late professor of physics - Dr. Horace Crater shows a template for something deeper and more profound. Note that the distance from Mound A to Mound E is 4,928 meters, approximately.

Journal of Space Exploration

Research | Vol 5 Iss 3

The Mounds of Cydonia: Elegant Geology, or Tetrahedral Geometry and Reactions of Pythagoras and Dirac?

Crater HW[1*], Mcdaniel SV[2] and Sirisena A[3]

[1]The University of Tennessee Space Institute, Tullahoma, TN 37388-9700, USA
[2]Department of Philosophy, Sonoma State University, Rohnert Park, California, USA
[3]Caversham, RG4 6UA, UK. (Former consultant with Symantec Corporation)

*Corresponding author: Crater HW, The University of Tennessee Space Institute, Tullahoma, TN 37388-9700, USA
ANANDALS@AOL.COM

Received: October 04, 2016; Accepted: November 10, 2016; Published: November 30, 2016

Abstract

Based on high resolution images from the ESA Mars express and NASA orbiter HiRise cameras, this paper gives new in-depth analysis of the remarkable geometric distribution of certain "mounds" or hill-like features in the Cydonia region of Mars. It validates the earlier measurements obtained using the lower resolution NASA Viking images, which hinted strongly at artificial surface interventions and adds new information regarding the geometry. We describe how those surface features, if artificial, provide an elegant and concise way for an intelligent species to transmit to another intelligence evidence that it understands the basics of tetrahedral geometry, prime numbers, and the quantum mechanics of the electrons spin, thereby giving additional evidence for the possibility of intelligent intervention. We also explore plausible geological explanations for the individual mounds and survey the possible natural mechanisms which may have been involved in their unusual and mathematically precise positioning.

The researchers

Dr. Horace W. Crater
Professor of Physics
University of TN Space Institute
Tullahoma, TN

Emeritus professor Stan McDaniel of Sonoma State University - California

Prepared by Ananda Sirisena

THE CHALLENGE BEFORE PARLIAMENT

Every member of Parliament needs to consider the following:

1) The sighting by Mr. and Mrs. Lewendon over AWE Burghfield on 11th September 2004

2) The proof provided by Dr. George King, Founder of the Aetherius Society about the Ural mountains nuclear accident in 1958 and the Windscale blunder in 1957.

3) The unusual finding on our Moon - Luna and the paper published in the Journal of Space Exploration.

4) The mathematical mystery on Mars analysed by professors Horace Crater and Stanley McDaniel, showing a precise mathematical fit to a square-root-two grid formation of six 'mounds'. Several scientific papers about this mystery have been published in peer-reviewed journals.

The reader is asked to ponder on the mysteries outlined in this book and approach their Member of Parliament in order to instigate a robust investigation

==
Lord Clancarty stated in 1979, after the House of Lords debate:

"In my speech in the Debate I mentioned that in February 1974, the then French Minister of Defence, Monsieur Robert Galley, was interviewed entirely about UFOs on France-Inter radio station. **Monsieur Galley stated that UFOs existed but freely admitted he did not know all the answers**. He said that the gendarmerie were taking part in investigating sightings and landings, as well as questioning witnesses and examining burnt circle marks on the ground."
==

References and further reading

THE NINE FREEDOMS – George King. The Aetherius Society, 1963

THE FLYING SAUCERS - A Report on the Flying Saucers, Their Crews and Their Mission to Earth - George King, The Aetherius Society, 1964

SCIENTIFIC STUDY OF UNIDENTIFIED FLYING OBJECTS – directed by E.U. Condon. University of Colorado, 1968

UFOs? YES! – Where The Condon Committee Went Wrong. David R. Saunders and R. Roger Harkins. Signet Books, 1968

ALIENS FROM SPACE by Donald Keyhoe, 1973.

UFOs and Nukes by Robert Hastings, 2008

UFOs and the Extraterrestrial Message by Richard Lawrence, 2010

UFOs - GENRALS, PILOTS AND GOVERNMENT OFFICIALS GO ON THE RECORD by Leslie Kean 2010

FLYING SAUCERS FROM BEYOND THE EARTH - A UFO Researcher's Odyssey by Gordon Lore, 2018

The author would like to thank and acknowledge the following:

Dr. George King
Dr. Zhores Medvedev
Professor Horace Crater
Professor Stanley McDaniel
Dr. Richard Lawrence
Dr. Mark Carlotto
Mr. Frank Warren
Mr. Francis Ridge
Mr. David Capraro
Mrs. Betty Lewendon
Mr. Michael Lewendon

NASA/JPL/ASU for planetary images

MASSIVE VIMANA OVER THE AWE

[Reconstruction by Michael Lewendon of object seen over the AWE on 11th September 2004]

The drawings made by Michael Lewendon do express the large size of the object seen over the AWE Burghfield.

Third edition, 2019

Printed in Great Britain
by Amazon